Japanese American Internment Camps

Other Books in the History Firsthand series:

The Civil War: The North
The Civil War: The South
The Great Depression
Sixties Counterculture

Japanese American Internment Camps

Bryan J. Grapes, *Book Editor*

David L. Bender, *Publisher*
Bruno Leone, *Executive Editor*
Bonnie Szumski, *Editorial Director*
Stuart B. Miller, *Managing Editor*
David M. Haugen, *Series Editor*

Greenhaven Press, Inc., San Diego, California

Every effort has been made to trace the owners of copyrighted material. The articles in this volume may have been edited for content, length, and/or reading level. The titles have been changed to enhance the editorial purpose.

Library of Congress Cataloging-in-Publication Data

Japanese American internment camps / Bryan J. Grapes, book editor
     p. cm. — (History firsthand)
    Includes bibliographical references and index.
    ISBN 0-7377-0412-8 (pbk. : alk. paper) —
    ISBN 0-7377-0413-6 (lib. : alk. paper)
    1. Japanese Americans—Evacuation and relocation, 1942–1945.
2. World War, 1939–1945—Japanese Americans. 3. Concentration
camps—United States. I. Grapes, Bryan J. II. Series.

D769.8.A6 J37   2001
940.53'089956073—dc21   00-037662
                                                       CIP

Cover photo: Bettmann/CORBIS
Library of Congress 39, 128
National Archives 14, 79, 121
National Japanese American Historical Society/
National Archives 22, 24, 51, 109, 142, 148, 157, 172

Copyright © 2001 by Greenhaven Press, Inc.
P.O. Box 289009 San Diego, CA 92198-9009

Printed in the USA

Contents

the Pacific coast. Since the Japanese represent a threat, they should be removed from coastal areas.

Chapter 2: The Internment of the Issei

duration of the war, leaving Ishii and her family to face the trying times after the Japanese attack without his guidance.

Chapter 3: Evacuation

how she offered comfort to Japanese residents who were distraught over the dismantling of their lives and communities.

Chapter 4: Life in the Camps

Chapter 5: Freedom

Foreword

In his preface to a book on the events leading to the Civil War, Stephen B. Oates, the historian and biographer of Abraham Lincoln, John Brown, and other noteworthy American historical figures, explained the difficulty of writing history in the traditional third-person voice of the biographer and historian. "The trouble, I realized, was the detached third-person voice," wrote Oates. "It seemed to wring all the life out of my characters and the antebellum era." Indeed, how can a historian, even one as prominent as Oates, compete with the eloquent voices of Daniel Webster, Abraham Lincoln, Harriet Beecher Stowe, Frederick Douglass, and Robert E. Lee?

Oates's comment notwithstanding, every student of history, professional and amateur alike, can name a score of excellent accounts written in the traditional third-person voice of the historian that bring to life an event or an era and the people who lived through it. In *Battle Cry of Freedom*, James M. McPherson vividly re-creates the American Civil War. Barbara Tuchman's *The Guns of August* captures in sharp detail the tensions in Europe that led to the outbreak of World War I. Taylor Branch's *Parting the Waters* provides a detailed and dramatic account of the American Civil Rights Movement. The study of history would be impossible without such guiding texts.

Nonetheless, Oates's comment makes a compelling point. Often the most convincing tellers of history are those who lived through the event, the eyewitnesses who recorded their firsthand experiences in autobiographies, speeches, memoirs, journals, and letters. The Greenhaven Press History Firsthand series presents history through the words of first-person narrators. Each text in this series captures a significant historical era or event—the American Civil War, the

Great Depression, the Holocaust, the Roaring 20s, the 1960s, the Vietnam War. Readers will investigate these historical eras and events by examining primary-source documents, authored by chroniclers both famous and little known. The texts in the History Firsthand series comprise the celebrated and familiar words of the presidents, generals, and famous men and women of letters who recorded their impressions for posterity, as well as the statements of the ordinary people who struggled to understand the storm of events around them—the foot soldiers who fought the great battles and their loved ones back home, the men and women who waited on the breadlines, the college students who marched in protest.

The texts in this series are particularly suited to students beginning serious historical study. By examining these firsthand documents, novice historians can begin to form their own insights and conclusions about the historical era or event under investigation. To aid the student in that process, the texts in the History Firsthand series include introductions that provide an overview of the era or event, timelines, and annotated bibliographies that point the serious student toward key historical works for further study.

The study of history commences with an examination of words—the testimony of witnesses who lived through an era or event and left for future generations the task of making sense of their accounts. The Greenhaven Press History Firsthand series invites the beginner historian to commence the process of historical investigation by focusing on the words of those individuals who made history by living through it and recording their experiences firsthand.

Introduction

America's Concentration Camps

On the morning of December 7, 1941, a large Japanese aircraft carrier strike force launched a surprise attack on the American Pacific Fleet at Pearl Harbor, Hawaii. The attack resulted in what many consider the worst defeat in U.S. military history. Five battleships and nine smaller warships were sunk and three other battleships were heavily damaged. One hundred eighty-eight planes were destroyed, most of them on the ground, and 2,403 people were killed. The attack virtually destroyed the American naval presence in the Pacific. Calling it a "day that will live in infamy," President Franklin D. Roosevelt presented a war message to Congress that fell just one vote short of unanimous approval. The attack did more than provide the impetus for America's entry into World War II, however. The destruction at Pearl Harbor triggered what John Tateishi described as "one of the most extraordinary episodes in the history of the country: The establishment of concentration camps in America."[1]

The attack on Pearl Harbor exacerbated long-entrenched anti-Asian prejudice in the United States, particularly on the West Coast. This anti-Asian sentiment, bolstered by accusations of "fifth column" activity by Japanese Americans from prominent western politicians and the press, proved influential in the U.S. government's decision to uproot 110,000 Japanese—two-thirds of them American citizens by birth—from their homes along the West Coast, and relocate them inland at remote camps surrounded by barbed wire and armed guards. It was a painful ordeal for so many people who considered themselves proud Americans.

The Japanese in America

The first Japanese immigrants arrived in America in the 1890s. Many of these first generation Japanese immigrants—called Issei—came to the United States for the same reasons that other immigrants had come in the past—freedom, economic opportunity, and the promise of a better life. Though welcomed as a cheap source of labor, the Issei were judged by the government to be incapable of assimilating into the American melting pot and denied the opportunity to apply for citizenship. In spite of being denied citizenship, the economic opportunities available in America proved to be a powerful lure for many Japanese, and by 1910 more than 125,000 Issei had settled in Hawaii and on the Pacific Coast of the United States.

Though the Japanese proved to be hard working and industrious people, their arrival on the West Coast immediately triggered resentment among their white neighbors. This resentment was given voice by a number of anti-Japanese organizations such as the Japanese Exclusion League, the Native Sons and Daughters of the Golden West, and the American Legion. Influenced by these organizations, politicians passed a number of laws aimed at limiting Japanese access to American prosperity, such as California's Anti-Alien Land Act of 1913, which prevented Issei from owning land, and the Gentlemen's Agreement of 1907, in which President Theodore Roosevelt severely restricted Japanese immigration to America. Japanese immigration to America was cut off completely when Congress passed the National Origins Act of 1924, which prevented immigration by aliens who were deemed ineligible for citizenship.

Despite the proliferation of anti-Asian sentiment, many Issei were thankful for the economic opportunities afforded them in America and a great number of them remained vigorously loyal to their adopted homeland. Yoshiko Uchida, a resident of Berkeley, California, in the days before World

War II describes her Issei father's admiration of America:

> My father cherished copies of the Declaration of Independence, the Bill of Rights, and the Constitution of the United States, and on national holidays he hung with great pride an enormous American flag on our front porch, even though at the time, this country declared the first generation Japanese immigrants to be "aliens ineligible for citizenship."[2]

The Nisei

Though the Issei were excluded from citizenship, their children—called Nisei—were American citizens by virtue of birth in the United States. The Issei, partly as a result of being excluded from American society, retained most of the customs and language of the old country and tried to pass them on to their children. The Nisei, however, were thoroughly American in culture (with the exception of a group called Kibei, who were sent to Japan for their education). They wore the same clothes as American children, spoke the

Japanese American school children in San Francisco recite the Pledge of Allegiance to the American flag. Despite anti-Asian feelings in America, both Issei and Nisei demonstrated great loyalty to their adopted country.

same language, played baseball, and attended the same schools. Yoshiko Uchida writes:

> In spite of the complete blending of Japanese qualities and values into our lives, neither my sister nor I, as children, ever considered ourselves anything other than Americans. At school we saluted the American flag and learned to become good citizens. All our teachers were white, as were many of our friends. Everything we read was in English, which was, of course, our native tongue.[3]

Despite their American ways, the Nisei were often subjected to the same prejudice as the Issei. Nisei students were denied places in law and medical schools and highly educated Japanese Americans often had to settle for jobs as houseboys and fruit stand workers.

Pearl Harbor

When Pearl Harbor was bombed, many Japanese Americans, both Issei and Nisei, reacted with the same shock and outrage as their white neighbors. Charles Kikuchi, a college student living in the San Francisco area, wrote in his diary:

> Pearl Harbor. We are at war! . . . The Japs bombed Hawaii and the entire fleet has been sunk. I just can't believe it. I don't know what . . . is going to happen to us, but we will all be called into the Army right away. . . . I will go and fight even if I think I am a coward and I don't believe in wars. . . . If we are ever going to prove our Americanism, this is the time.[4]

Nisei lined up to volunteer for the armed forces and Japanese Americans, eager to prove their loyalty to the United States, prepared to support the war effort along with their fellow countrymen. Japanese Americans bought war bonds, joined the Red Cross, and volunteered for civilian defense patrols. As they were preparing to support their country, however, many Japanese Americans wondered how their white neighbors would react to them. In her memoir, *Nisei Daughter*, Monica Sone, a resident of Seattle, Washington, in the opening days of World War II recalls an exchange between two friends: "'What a spot to be in! Do you think

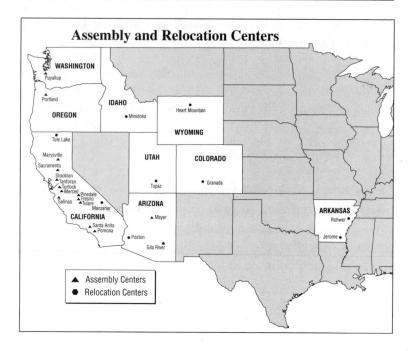

we'll be considered Japanese or Americans?' A boy replied quietly, 'We'll be Japs, same as always.'"[5]

The Issei were much more apprehensive than the Nisei of white reaction following the bombing of Pearl Harbor. When war was declared, the Issei, along with a number of Italian and German residents, were classified as "enemy aliens" by the U.S. government. Many Issei hastily destroyed family heirlooms brought from Japan—samurai swords, flags, Japanese books—fearing that they might be viewed by the authorities as evidence of loyalty to the Japanese emperor. Jeanne Wakatsuki Houston, a resident of Ocean Park, California, recalls the night her family learned of the Japanese attack:

> That night Papa burned the flag he had brought with him from Hiroshima thirty-five years earlier. It was such a beautiful piece of material, I couldn't believe he was doing that. He burned a lot of papers too, documents, anything that might suggest he still had some connection with Japan.[6]

Despite destroying all evidence that might have indicated ties or loyalty to Japan, the FBI, authorized by President Roosevelt and Attorney General Francis Biddle, swept through numerous Japanese communities rounding up enemy aliens that were deemed dangerous to the security of the United States. Most of the men detained were prominent businessmen, community leaders, and members of Japanese social organizations. A great number of Issei fishermen were detained as well—suspected of making contact with enemy ships while at sea. In many cases children came home from school to find the FBI ransacking their homes and questioning their parents. Some fathers were taken into custody by the FBI after their searches were concluded. "When I got home, the house was filled with an uneasy quiet. A strange man sat in our living room and my father was gone. The FBI had come to pick him up, as they had dozens of other Japanese men,"[7] writes Yoshiko Uchida. Along with some West Coast alien residents of Italian and German ancestry, Uchida's father was sent to Missoula, Montana, and incarcerated in one of four Justice Department camps for enemy aliens. Families sometimes waited for months for word from husbands, fathers, and brothers that were held by the Justice Department. When they were finally allowed to communicate, it was only through heavily censored letters and telegrams. Most of the men held in these camps were eventually cleared of any wrongdoing and allowed to rejoin their families (who by this time were being sent to camps themselves). Others who were judged disloyal to the United States were held for eventual deportation back to Japan.

The Role of the Media

The Japanese victory at Pearl Harbor had been so swift and decisive that many in the United States came to believe that Japanese forces were aided by "fifth column" saboteurs of Japanese ancestry. The notion that fifth column activity on the West Coast was a reality was reinforced by comments made by respected columnists and radio journalists across the United States. Many charged that all Japanese living on the Pacific shore, aliens and citizens alike, were a secret army planted by the Japanese government, loyal only to the Japanese emperor and poised to strike at his command. Los Angeles radio commentator John B. Hughes estimated that 90 percent of American-born Japanese were loyal to the country of their parents' birth and that they would "die joyously for the honor of Japan."[8] Moreover, the media charged, the Nisei were a more insidious threat to the safety of the West Coast than the Issei because American-born Japanese were well versed in the customs and the language of the United States, making it easier for them to commit sabotage. Calls for the removal of all Japanese residents from the West Coast became rampant. Columnist Henry McLemore wrote:

> I am for immediate removal of every Japanese on the West Coast to a point deep in the interior. Herd 'em up, pack 'em off and give 'em the inside room in the badlands. Let 'em be pinched, hurt, hungry, and dead against it. . . . Personally, I hate the Japanese. And that goes for all of them.[9]

Politicians Join the Fight

In addition to the media, prominent West Coast politicians soon lent their voices to the chorus of those calling for the evacuation of Japanese Americans. California governor Culbert Olson, Attorney General Earl Warren (later to become chief justice of the United States), Los Angeles mayor Fletcher Bowron, and General John DeWitt, head of the army's Western Defense Command, agitated for the removal of Japanese Americans from the Pacific Coast. Warren called the presence of Japanese Americans on the Pacific shore the "Achilles heel" of the civilian defense effort. Echoing Warren's sentiment in his testimony before the Tolan Committee (a committee created by Congress to investigate the threat of enemy alien activity on the West Coast) Earl Riley, mayor of Portland, Oregon, stated that the Nisei "are definitely a hazard, and that the longer they are permitted to have the freedom that they now have . . . the greater is the hazard that is created for our defense situation."[10]

The sentiments exhibited by politicians like Warren and

Riley ran contrary to the findings of Curtis B. Munson, a special representative of the State Department who conducted a study of the degree of danger posed by the Issei and the Nisei living on the West Coast in the months prior to Pearl Harbor, when relations between the United States and Japan began to deteriorate. "As interview after interview piled up," Munson recorded, "those bringing in results began to call it the same old tune. . . . There is no Japanese 'problem' on the Coast. There will be no armed uprising of Japanese."[11]

On February 19, 1942, despite evidence of their loyalty to the United States contained in the Munson report, President Roosevelt authorized the removal of all Japanese from the West Coast, citizen and alien, when he signed Executive Order 9066. The order gave General DeWitt the authority to remove Japanese Americans from sensitive military areas in the western portion of the United States.

The Civilian Exclusion Orders

In March 1942 General DeWitt designated the western halves of Washington, Oregon, California, and the southern half of Arizona as Military Area Number One, an area from which Japanese could be removed. A 9:00 P.M. to 6:00 A.M. curfew was imposed upon Japanese living within Military Area Number One, and Japanese residents were not allowed to travel more than five miles from their homes. They were also ordered to surrender contraband items such as binoculars, cameras, maps, and short wave radios.

Shortly after the travel restrictions were placed upon them, Japanese residents were informed that they were to be removed from Military Area Number One. They were initially encouraged to relocate on their own and as many as three thousand Japanese took advantage of contacts and relatives in the midwest and on the East Coast. For many Japanese, however, the West Coast was the only home they had ever known and they did not have relatives or friends outside of the communities where they lived. By the end of March 1942 over 100,000 Japanese remained in Military Area Number One and DeWitt was forced to conclude that voluntary relocation was a failure. He ordered all Japanese to remain in place until the army could implement an orderly evacuation.

Throughout the spring of 1942 General DeWitt issued a series of Civilian Exclusion Orders instructing Japanese residents of Military Area Number One to prepare for evacuation. Evacuees were told to pack only what they could carry and to make arrangements for the care or sale of personal items that could not be taken. In many cases, families were given as little as one week to dispose of a lifetime's collection of personal belongings. Unscrupulous buyers took advantage of desperate Japanese who needed to sell what they could not carry. "The secondhand dealers had been prowling around for weeks, like wolves, offering humiliating prices for goods and furniture they knew many of us would have to sell sooner or later,"[12] Jeanne Wakatsuki Houston recalls. Barry Saiki, a resident of Stockton, California, writes:

> Our 1939 Dodge, with five brand new tires, fetched $400 and our restaurant chinaware, cutlery, and refrigerators netted several hundred dollars. The two weeks before May 20 [evacuation day] were chaotic as the family sorted the accumulation of the preceding decades into the two suitcases allowed each person. Some families owning homes boarded them up, hoping that they would not be vandalized during their absence.[13]

Ironically, Japanese Americans in Hawaii were never relocated, even though Hawaii was much closer to the theater of war in the Pacific and in possession of a larger Japanese population than the West Coast. Japanese Americans were judged too important to the local economy to be moved. Many point to the Hawaiian Japanese as proof that the decision to evacuate Japanese residents from the West Coast was based on racism, not military necessity.

The Assembly Centers

Following the liquidation of their personal assets, Japanese residents were placed on buses or trains, escorted by armed guards, to one of twelve temporary reception centers, officially known as assembly centers. Many of these assembly centers were hastily converted racetracks and fairgrounds where Japanese families were sometimes housed in old horse stalls. These hastily constructed apartments were drafty and not well suited to privacy. The walls were paper-thin and in most cases did not reach all the way to the ceiling. The quarters were cramped and poorly ventilated, and as Yoshiko Uchida describes, still carried reminders of their previous occupants:

> The stall was about ten by twenty feet and empty except for three folded Army cots lying on the floor. Dust, dirt, and wood shaving covered the linoleum that had been laid over manure-covered boards, the smell of horses hung in the air, and the whitened corpses of many insects still clung to the hastily white-washed walls.[14]

Evacuees also found appalling sanitary conditions in the mess halls of the assembly centers. Swarms of flies infested the kitchens and food was improperly handled and stored. As a result, hundreds of residents suffered severe cases of food poisoning. Despite the unsanitary conditions and the lack of privacy, the evacuees settled into their new homes and began to adjust to their surroundings. Just as the evacuees began to adjust, however, orders were issued to prepare for transfer to the permanent relocation camps. Between June and October of 1942, residents were transferred to one of ten relocation camps administered by the War Relocation Authority (WRA), a civilian agency established by President Roosevelt to supervise the resettlement of Japanese evacuees.

The Relocation Centers

The relocation centers were built in the barren desert areas of California, Arizona, Idaho, Utah, Wyoming, and Arkansas. Evacuees arrived to find bare, military style compounds that were as sparsely furnished as the assembly centers—just a few cots and a pot-bellied stove for warmth. In most cases, inner walls and ceilings had yet to be built. Most of the camps were located in areas that were subject to drastic tem-

Military police stand duty in a watchtower at the Santa Anita assembly center in April 1942. Many relocation camps like this one were previously racetracks, hastily adapted to house Japanese Americans.

perature shifts and evacuees who were accustomed to the mild climate of California had to endure temperatures that climbed to over 100 degrees during the day, and dropped to near freezing at night. Most of these camps were also subject to severe, blinding dust storms, which coated everything in camp, inside and out, in a fine layer of dust. Monica Sone remembers the dusty greeting she and her fellow evacuees received upon their arrival at Camp Minidoka in Idaho:

> On our first day in camp, we were given a rousing welcome by a dust storm. . . . We felt as if we were standing in a gigantic sand-mixing machine as the sixty-mile gale lifted the loose earth up into the sky, obliterating everything. Sand filled our mouths and nostrils and stung our faces and hands like a thousand darting needles. . . . At last we staggered into our room, gasping and blinded. . . . The window panes rattled madly, and the dust poured in through the cracks like smoke.[15]

The evacuees eventually began to conquer the harsh elements and bleak conditions in many of the camps. Many internees fashioned furniture and partitions for their apartments from scrap lumber provided by the WRA. Professional farmers and gardeners among the evacuees transformed the barren desert landscape into fertile farmland and attractive oriental gardens. One by one, the organizations and social institutions that had been a part of Japanese American life on the West Coast, such as schools, churches, libraries, police and fire departments, movie theaters, and Boy Scout troops, were resurrected. Many camps were allowed to elect camp governments, although the WRA stipulated that the Issei, since they were not citizens, could not be elected to office. Many of the relocation camps were soon indistinguishable from other small towns in America, except for the armed sentries and barbed wire fences.

Political Tension

While many internees did their best to reproduce the communities they lived in on the Pacific shore, the corrosive nature of camp life soon became evident. The Japanese family unit began to break down as a result of the crowded lifestyle of the camps and frayed nerves easily succumbed to anger. Families no longer ate together in the mess hall atmosphere of the camps. Children preferred to eat with their more Americanized friends and older generation Issei retreated into their own groups.

The political divide between the Nisei and Issei solidified as controversial debates were introduced. In January 1943 the subject of military service was the cause of a great deal of tension between Nisei sons and Issei parents. In the wake of the attack on Pearl Harbor all Japanese Americans were classified 4-C by the U.S. Army. This was the same designation given to enemy aliens and it made the Nisei ineligible for military service. Those Nisei who were already in the armed services were either discharged or assigned menial tasks. In January of 1943 President Roosevelt restored the privilege of volunteering for military service to the Nisei and the government began to actively recruit Japanese Americans for an all-Nisei combat team. Many Nisei, influenced by the views of the Japanese American Citizens League (JACL), were still eager to prove their loyalty to the United States and felt that military service was the best way to do it. Many Issei, however, objected to their sons fighting for a country that stripped them of their rights and put them behind a barbed wire fence. "Is this what we deserve from our children," one Issei woman argued, "after years and years of work and hardship for their sake? Ah, we've bred nothing but fools! They can be insulted, their parents insulted, and still they volunteer. The Nisei never had backbones!"[16] To this Tom Kawaguichi answered:

> In the 442nd [Regimental Combat Team], a lot of us felt that this was our only chance to demonstrate our loyalty; we would never get a second chance—this was it. We saw the treatment that we were getting and we wanted there to be no question about what we were and where we were going.[17]

In January 1943, President Roosevelt decided to accept Japanese American volunteers into the armed forces. Many Nisei volunteered, partly to prove their loyalty to the country. Here members of the all–Japanese American D Company, 100th infantry, march in Italy.

Despite threats from parents and pro-Japanese militants, hundreds of Nisei volunteered to serve in the 442nd Regimental Combat Team, an all Nisei unit which saw action in North Africa, Italy, and France and became one of the most decorated units of the war.

The Loyalty Questionnaire

In a number of camps pro-Japanese Issei and Kibei made threats against Nisei who they felt were too conciliatory toward camp officials and the U.S. government. Relations between the factions worsened yet again when the WRA began to administer a loyalty questionnaire to all internees over the age of seventeen. The controversy centered on questions 27 and 28 of the questionnaire. Question 27, directed at draft-age males, asked: "Are you willing to serve in the armed forces of the United States on combat duty, wherever ordered?" Women were asked if they would serve in the Women's Army Corps (WACS) or the Army Nurse Corps. Question 28, directed at all internees, asked:

> Will you swear unqualified allegiance to the United States of America and faithfully defend the United States from any or all attack by foreign or domestic forces, and forswear any form of allegiance or obedience to the Japanese emperor, or any other foreign government, power, or organization?

Many felt that answering "yes" to both questions was the best possible solution, even if it meant exposing oneself to the draft. A "yes-yes" answer was also the best way to demonstrate to the government that Japanese Americans were loyal, law-abiding citizens deserving of better treatment. A "no-no" answer meant certain deportation to Japan at the war's end. Militant Kibei and Issei, however, were determined not to swear loyalty to the country that had them incarcerated. Also, some Issei worried that a "yes-yes" answer would leave them as people without a country. Since they were not American citizens, if they renounced Japan and the American government chose to deport them anyway, they would have nowhere to go. A small group of Nisei believed that 28 was a loaded question. If they renounced allegiance to the emperor, it would imply that they had allegiance to the emperor in the first place. Some Nisei wondered if they might be judged disloyal if they answered yes to question 28.

Numerous physical clashes occurred between the groups and the militants who answered "no-no" were eventually transferred to a segregation camp for disloyal internees at Tule Lake, California. Most were deported back to Japan after the war.

Legal Challenges

Though the relocation of Japanese Americans remained relatively unchallenged (the JACL encouraged Japanese to comply with evacuation orders, believing it was the best way to demonstrate loyalty), a few Japanese Americans did challenge the legality of Executive Order 9066 in the courts. The two most prominent cases were those of Fred Korematsu and Mitsuye Endo. In 1942 Fred Korematsu, a welder who refused to leave his home in San Leandro, California, was arrested for violating the exclusion order. Korematsu, with help from the American Civil Liberties Union (ACLU) in Northern California, challenged the government's policy on the grounds that the government had no right to remove and imprison a race of people because of their ancestry. In 1944 the Supreme Court upheld Korematsu's conviction by a 6–3 vote, ruling that Korematsu was not excluded because of his race. The tribunal concluded that he

> was excluded because we are at war with the Japanese Empire, because the properly constituted military authorities feared an invasion of our West Coast and felt constrained to take proper security measures, because they decided that the military urgency of the situation demanded that all citizens of Japanese ancestry be segregated from the West Coast temporarily.[18]

Mitsuye Endo, a civil servant who was evacuated to the Tule Lake center, based her challenge to the relocation on the argument that the government had no right to detain loyal citizens without just cause. Endo filed a writ of habeas corpus, which compelled the government to release her or to give just cause as to why she should be detained. In 1944 the Supreme Court ruled in favor of Endo and declared that "whatever power the War Relocation Authority may have to detain other classes of citizens, it has no authority to (detain) citizens who are . . . loyal."[19] As a result of this ruling, the government announced that it would eradicate its policy of internment for loyal Japanese Americans in December 1944.

The WRA had already begun to release select internees as early as October of 1942. Those released early in the war, however, were not allowed to return to the West Coast. The Supreme Court's decision in *Endo v. United States* opened the door for Japanese Americans to go back home to start their lives anew.

Redress

At the close of the war most Japanese Americans were eager to forget their ordeal in the camps and set themselves to the task of rebuilding their lives. Naturalization laws were loosened at the close of the war and in 1952 many of the Issei that were interned were allowed to apply for citizenship, which most did. The Japanese American community then settled into the task of rebuilding their neighborhoods as law-abiding citizens. The episode was widely forgotten over the next decades and no mention was made of it in history books.

In 1980, at the behest of the JACL, Congress created the Commission on Wartime Relocation and Internment of Civilians to review the circumstances surrounding Executive Order 9066. The Commission's report, entitled *Personal Justice Denied,* concluded that the actions taken against Japanese Americans by the military and President Roosevelt were not justified. Moreover, the report stated:

> The broad historical causes which shaped these decisions were race prejudice, war hysteria, and a failure of political leadership. . . . A grave injustice was done to American citizens and resident aliens of Japanese ancestry who, without individual review or any probative evidence against them, were excluded, removed and detained by the United States during World War II.[20]

The Commission recommended that restitution in the amount of $20,000 be made to each of the survivors of the relocation. In October 1990, former internees received a letter of apology from President George Bush, which read:

> A monetary sum and words alone cannot restore the lost years or erase painful memories; neither can they fully convey our Nation's resolve to rectify injustice and to uphold the rights of individuals. We can never fully right the wrongs of the past. But we can take a clear stand for justice and recognize that serious injustices were done to Japanese Americans during World War II.
>
> In enacting a law calling for restitution and offering a sincere apology, your fellow Americans have, in a very real sense, renewed their traditional commitment to the ideals of freedom, equality, and justice. You and your family have our best wishes for the future.[21]

Shortly after President Bush issued this apology, the first reparations checks were mailed to the survivors of America's concentration camps.

Notes

1. John Tateishi, *And Justice for All: An Oral History of the Japanese American Detention Camps.* Seattle: University of Washington Press, 1984, p. xiii.

2. Yoshiko Uchida, *Desert Exile: The Uprooting of a Japanese American Family.* Seattle: University of Washington Press, 1982, p. 6.

3. Uchida, *Desert Exile,* pp. 36, 40.

4. John Modell, ed., *The Kikuchi Diary: Chronicle from an American Concentration Camp: The Tanforan Journals of Charles Kikuchi.* Urbana: University of Illinois Press, 1973, pp. 42–43.

5. Monica Sone, *Nisei Daughter.* Boston: Little, Brown, 1953, p. 146.

6. Jeanne Wakatsuki Houston and James D. Houston, *Farewell to Manzanar.* New York: Bantam Books, 1973, p. 5.

7. Uchida, *Desert Exile,* p. 46.

8. Quoted in Roger Daniels, Sandra C. Taylor, and Harry H.L. Kitano, eds., *Japanese Americans: From Relocation to Redress.* Salt Lake City: University of Utah Press, 1986, p. 80.

9. Quoted in Daniels, Taylor, and Kitano, *Japanese Americans: From Relocation to Redress,* p. 80.

10. Earl Riley, in House Select Committee Investigating National Defense Migration, *National Defense Migration: Hearings on H.R. 113,* 77th Congress, 2nd session, February 26 and 28, and March 2, 1942, p. 11305.

11. Quoted in Michi Weglyn, *Years of Infamy: The Untold Story of America's Concentration Camps.* New York: Morrow Quill, 1976, p. 45.

12. Wakatsuki Houston and Houston, *Farewell to Manzanar,* p. 10.

13. Daniels, Taylor, and Kitano, *Japanese Americans: From Relocation to Redress,* pp. 16–17.

14. Uchida, *Desert Exile*, p. 70.

15. Sone, *Nisei Daughter*, p. 192.

16. Sone, *Nisei Daughter*, p. 201.

17. Tateishi, *And Justice for All,* p. 184.

18. William Dudley, ed., *World War II: Opposing Viewpoints.* San Diego: Greenhaven, 1997, p. 220.

19. Quoted in Diane Yancey, *Life in a Japanese American Internment Camp.* San Diego: Lucent Books, 1998, p. 74.

20. Quoted in Daniels, Taylor, and Kitano, *Japanese Americans: From Relocation to Redress*, p. 5.

21. Yancey, *Life in a Japanese Internment Camp,* p. 96.

Chapter 1

The Arguments for Relocation

Chapter Preface

In the days following the destruction of the U.S. Pacific Fleet at Pearl Harbor, Hawaii, many military officials and West Coast residents braced themselves for a Japanese attack on the Pacific coast. Their fears were not completely unfounded. The West Coast's main line of defense was sent to the bottom of Pearl Harbor by planes from a large Japanese aircraft carrier strike force that was now roaming the Pacific Ocean unopposed. An attack on the defenseless West Coast appeared imminent and the threat of an invasion sparked a wave of intense anti-Asian sentiment in California, Oregon, and Washington.

Reasoning that the 110,000 residents of Japanese ancestry living on the West Coast might prove friendly to a Japanese invasion force, many prominent journalists, military officials, and politicians began to agitate for their removal. The press teemed with stories about "fifth column" saboteurs aiding in the destruction at Pearl Harbor. Most prominent among the journalists who alleged Japanese American cooperation with the enemy was respected syndicated columnist Walter Lippmann. His article of February 13, 1942, entitled "The Fifth Column on the Coast," which appeared in newspapers across the country, warned that the West Coast was in "imminent danger of a combined attack from within and from without." Lippmann's column and several others contributed greatly to the rising tide of anti-Japanese hysteria.

Lieutenant General John L. DeWitt, head of the Western Defense Command, also proved to be influential in convincing the government to remove Japanese Americans from the Pacific coast. "The very fact that no sabotage has taken place to date is a disturbing and confirming indication that such action will be taken," General DeWitt argued in a report he submitted to Secretary of War Henry L. Stimson on February 14, 1942. On February 19, President Roosevelt signed Executive Order 9066, authorizing General DeWitt to remove all Japanese Americans from sensitive military areas.

Shortly after General DeWitt submitted his recommendations to the secretary of war, Congress created the Tolan Committee to investigate the threat of enemy alien activity on the West Coast. Numerous politicians such as San Francisco mayor Angelo J. Rossi and California attorney general Earl Warren appeared before the Tolan Committee and argued passionately for the removal of all Japanese Americans, regardless of citizenship, from the coastal areas. Such arguments proved to be instrumental in the removal of the entire Japanese community from the Pacific coast.

The Fifth Column on the Coast

Walter Lippmann

After the Japanese attack on the American Pacific Fleet in
Pearl Harbor, Hawaii, stories about possible fifth column
cooperation among the Japanese Americans living in Hawaii
proliferated in the American press. In the following editorial,
nationally syndicated journalist Walter Lippmann argues that
the West Coast, with its large population of Japanese Americans, was particularly vulnerable to this kind of attack. Reasoning that the entire west coast had become a battle zone,
Lippmann argues that the movement of Japanese Americans
should be severely restricted.

The enemy alien problem on the Pacific Coast, or much
more accurately the fifth column problem, is very serious and it is very special. What makes it so serious and so
special is that the Pacific Coast is in imminent danger of a
combined attack from within and from without. The danger
is not, as it would be in the inland centers or perhaps even
for the present on the Atlantic Coast, from sabotage alone.
The peculiar danger of the Pacific Coast is in a Japanese raid
accompanied by enemy action inside American territory.
This combination can be very formidable indeed. For while
the striking power of Japan from the sea and air might not
in itself be overwhelming at any one point just now, Japan
cold strike a blow which might do irreparable damage if it
were accompanied by the kind of organized sabotage to

Reprinted from "The Fifth Column on the Coast," by Walter Lippmann, *Los Angeles
Times*, February 12, 1942.

which this part of the country is specially vulnerable.

This is a sober statement of the situation, in fact a report, based not on speculation but on what is known to have taken place and to be taking place in this area of the war. It is the fact that the Japanese navy has been reconnoitering the Pacific Coast more or less continually and for a considerable period of time, testing and feeling out the American defenses. It is the fact that communication takes place between the enemy at seas and enemy agents on land. These are facts which we shall ignore or minimize at our peril. It also is the fact that since the outbreak of the Japanese war there has been no important sabotage on the Pacific Coast. From what we know about Hawaii and about the fifth column in Europe, this is not, as some have liked to think, a sign that there is nothing to be feared. It is a sign that the blow is well organized and that it is held back until it can be struck with maximum effect.

Realism Needed

In preparing to repel the attack the Army and Navy have all the responsibility, but they are facing it with one hand tied down in Washington. I am sure I understand fully and appreciate thoroughly the unwillingness of Washington to adopt a policy of mass evacuation and mass internment of all those who are technically enemy aliens. But I submit that Washington is not defining the problem on the Pacific Coast correctly and that therefore it is raising insoluble issues unnecessarily and failing to deal with the practical issues promptly. No one ever can hope to get the right answer unless he first asks the right questions.

The official approach to the danger is through a series of unrealities. There is the assumption that it is a problem of "enemy aliens." As a matter of fact it is certainly also a problem of native-born American citizens. There is the assumption that a citizen may not be interfered with unless he has committed an overt act, or at least unless there is strong evidence that he is about to commit an overt act. There is the assumption that if the rights of a citizen are abridged anywhere they have been abridged everywhere. The effect of assumptions has been to precipitate legalistic and ideological arguments between the military authorities out here and the civil authorities in Washington, and between the aroused citizenry of the Coast and their fellow countrymen in the interior.

A much simpler approach will, I believe, yield much more practical results. Forget for a moment all about enemy aliens, dual citizenship, naturalized citizens, native citizens of enemy alien parentage and consider a warship in San Francisco Harbor, an air plant in Los Angeles, a general's headquarters at Oshkosh and an admiral's at Podunk. Then think of the lineal descendant. If there happened to be such a person, of George Washington, the Father of his Country, and consider what happens to Mr. Washington if he decides he would like to visit the warship, or take a walk in the airplane plant, or to drop in and photograph the general and the admiral in their quarters.

He is stopped by the sentry. He has to prove who he is. He has to prove that he has a good reason for doing what he wishes to do. He has to register, sign papers and wear an identification button. Then perhaps, if he proves his case, he is escorted by an armed guard while he does his errand and until he has checked out of the place and his papers and his button have been returned. Have Mr. Washington's constitutional rights been abridged? Has he been denied the dignity of the human person? Has his loyalty been impugned?

Proof Needed

Now, it seems to me that this is in principle and in general the procedure which ought to be used for all persons in a zone which the military authorities regard as open to enemy attack. In that zone, as in the corridors of the general's headquarters or on the deck of the warship or within the gates of the airplane plant, everyone should be compelled to prove that he has a good reason for being there, and no one should be allowed to come and go until he has proved that his business is necessary and consistent with the national defense.

In the vital and vulnerable areas it should be the rule that residence, employment, communication by telephone, telegraph, automobile and railroad are confined to licensed persons who are fully identified and whose activities are fully known to the authorities and to their neighbors. The Pacific Coast is officially a combat zone; some part of it may at any moment be a battlefield. Nobody's constitutional rights include the right to reside and do business on a battlefield. And nobody ought to be on a battlefield who has no good reason for being there.

What Washington has been trying to find is a policy for dealing with all enemy aliens everywhere and all potential fifth columnists everywhere. Yet a policy which may be wise in most parts of the country may be extremely foolhardy in a combat zone. Therefore, much the best thing to do is to recognize the western combat zone as a territory quite different from the rest of the country, and then to set up in that zone a special regime. This has been done on the Bataan Peninsula, in Hawaii, in Alaska, in the Canal Zone. Why not also on the threatened West Coast of the United States?

Japanese Americans Constitute a Dangerous Threat to Security

Earl Warren

California attorney general Earl Warren was one of the most prominent proponents of Japanese relocation. In the following essay, excerpted from his testimony before the Tolan Committee, a Congressional commission investigating problems posed by enemy aliens living along the Pacific shore, Warren argues that Japanese Americans, as potential saboteurs, pose a serious threat to the safety of the west coast. The children of first generation Japanese immigrants, American citizens by birth, constitute an even greater threat than Japanese aliens, Warren contends, because this larger segment of the Japanese population has been educated in Japan and thereby subject to Japanese militarist doctrine. Moreover, Warren points out, relocation would benefit Japanese Americans by protecting them from vigilantism.

For some time I have been of the opinion that the solution of our alien enemy problem with all its ramifications, which include the descendants of aliens, is not only a Federal problem but is a military problem. We believe that all of the decisions in that regard must be made by the military command that is charged with the security of this area. I am

Excerpted from Earl Warren's testimony before the U.S. House Select Committee Investigating National Defense Migration, Washington, D.C., February 21, 23, 1942.

convinced that the fifth-column activities of our enemy call for the participation of people who are in fact American citizens, and that if we are to deal realistically with the problem we must realize that we will be obliged in time of stress to deal with subversive elements of our own citizenry.

If that be true, it creates almost an impossible situation for the civil authorities because the civil authorities cannot take protective measures against people of that character. We may suspect their loyalty. We may even have some evidence or, perhaps, substantial evidence of their disloyalty. But until we have the whole pattern of the enemy plan, until we are able to go into court and beyond the exclusion of a reasonable doubt establish the guilt of those elements among our American citizens, there is no way that civil government can cope with the situation.

On the other hand, we believe that in an area, such as in California, which has been designated as a combat zone, when things have happened such as have happened here on the coast, something should be done and done immediately. We believe that any delay in the adoption of the necessary protective measures is to invite disaster. It means that we, too, will have in California a Pearl Harbor incident.

I believe that up to the present and perhaps for a long time to come the greatest danger to continental United States is that from well organized sabotage and fifth-column activity.

Opportunities for Sabotage

California presents, perhaps, the most likely objective in the Nation for such activities. There are many reasons why that is true. First, the size and number of our naval and military establishments in California would make it attractive to our enemies as a field of sabotage. Our geographical position with relation to our enemy and to the war in the Pacific is also a tremendous factor. The number and the diversification of our war industries is extremely vital. The fire hazards due to our climate, our forest areas, and the type of building construction make us very susceptible to fire sabotage. Then the tremendous number of aliens that we have

After the surprise air invasion of Pearl Harbor by Japan, many Americans were concerned that the California coast would be next.

resident here makes it almost an impossible problem from the standpoint of law enforcement.

A wave of organized sabotage in California accompanied by an actual air raid or even by a prolonged black-out could not only be more destructive to life and property but could result in retarding the entire war effort of this Nation far more than the treacherous bombing of Pearl Harbor.

I hesitate to think what the result would be of the destruction of any of our big airplane factories in this State. It will interest you to know that some of our airplane factories in this State are entirely surrounded by Japanese land ownership or occupancy. It is a situation that is fraught with the greatest danger and under no circumstances should it ever be permitted to exist.

I have some maps here that will show the specific instances of that character. In order to advise the committee more accurately on this subject I have asked the various district attorneys throughout the State to submit maps to me showing every Japanese ownership and occupancy in the State. Those maps tell a story, a story that is not very heartening to anyone who has the responsibility of protecting life and property either in time of peace or in war.

To assume that the enemy has not planned fifth column activities for us in a wave of sabotage is simply to live in a fool's paradise. These activities, whether you call them "fifth column activities" or "sabotage" or "war behind the lines upon civilians," or whatever you may call it, are just as much an integral part of Axis warfare as any of their military and naval operations. When I say that I refer to all of the Axis powers with which we are at war.

It has developed into a science and a technique that has been used most effectively against every nation with which the Axis powers are at war. It has been developed to a degree almost beyond the belief of our American citizens. That is one of the reasons it is so difficult for our people to become aroused and appreciate the danger of such activities. Those activities are now being used actively in the war in the Pacific, in every field of operations about which I have read. They have unquestionably, gentlemen, planned such activities for California. For us to believe to the contrary is just not realistic.

Unfortunately, however, many of our people and some of our authorities and, I am afraid, many of our people in other parts of the country are of the opinion that because we have had no sabotage and no fifth column activities in this State since the beginning of the war, that means that none have been planned for us. But I take the view that that is the most ominous sign in our whole situation. It convinces me more than perhaps any other factor that the sabotage that we are to get, the fifth column activities that we are to get, are timed just like Pearl Harbor was timed and just like the invasion of France, and of Denmark, and of Norway, and all of those other countries.

Invisible Deadline for Sabotage

I believe that we are just being lulled into a false sense of security and that the only reason we haven't had disaster in

California is because it has been timed for a different date, and that when that time comes if we don't do something about it it is going to mean disaster both to California and to our Nation. Our day of reckoning is bound to come in that regard. When, nobody knows, of course, but we are approaching an invisible deadline.

The Chairman [Rep. John Tolan]: On that point, when that came up in our committee hearings there was not a single case of sabotage reported on the Pacific coast, we heard the heads of the Navy and the Army, and they all tell us that the Pacific coast can be attacked. The sabotage would come coincident with that attack, would it not?

Attorney General Warren: Exactly.

The Chairman: They would be fools to tip their hands now, wouldn't they?

Attorney General Warren: Exactly. If there were sporadic sabotage at this time or if there had been for the last 2 months, the people of California or the Federal authorities would be on the alert to such an extent that they could not possibly have any real fifth column activities when the M-day comes. And I think that that should figure very largely in our conclusions on this subject.

Approaching an invisible deadline as we do, it seems to me that no time can be wasted in making the protective measures that are essential to the security of this State. And when I say "this State" I mean all of the coast, of course. I believe that Oregon and Washington are entitled to the same sort of consideration as the zone of danger as California. Perhaps our danger is intensified by the number of our industries and the number of our aliens, but it is much the same. . . .

American-Born Japanese

I want to say that the consensus of opinion among the law-enforcement officers of this State is that there is more potential danger among the group of Japanese who are born in this country than from the alien Japanese who were born in Japan. That might seem an anomaly to some people, but the fact is that, in the first place, there are twice as many of them. There are 33,000 aliens and there are 66,000 born in this country.

In the second place, most of the Japanese who were born in Japan are over 55 years of age. There has been practically no migration to this country since 1924. But in some instances the children of those people have been sent to Japan for their education, either in whole or in part, and while they are over there they are indoctrinated with the idea of Japanese imperialism. They receive their religious instruction which ties up their religion with their Emperor, and they come back here imbued with the ideas and the policies of Imperial Japan.

While I do not cast a reflection on every Japanese who is born in this country—of course we will have loyal ones—I do say that the consensus of opinion is that taking the groups by and large there is more potential danger to this State from the group that is born here than from the group that is born in Japan.

Mr. Arnold [Rep. Laurence Arnold]: Let me ask you a question at this point.

Attorney General Warren: Yes, Congressman.

Mr. Arnold: Do you have any way of knowing whether any one of this group that you mention is loyal to this country or loyal to Japan?

Attorney General Warren: Congressman, there is no way that we can establish that fact. We believe that when we are dealing with the Caucasian race we have methods that will test the loyalty of them, and we believe that we can, in dealing with the Germans and the Italians, arrive at some fairly sound conclusions because of our knowledge of the way they live in the community and have lived for many years. But when we deal with the Japanese we are in an entirely different field and we cannot form any opinion that we believe to be sound. Their method of living, their language, make for this difficulty. Many of them who show you a birth certificate stating that they were born in this State, perhaps, or born in Honolulu, can hardly speak the English language because, although they were born here, when they were 4 or

5 years of age they were sent over to Japan to be educated and they stayed over there through their adolescent period at least, and then they came back here thoroughly Japanese.

The Chairman: There are certain Japanese schools here, are there not?

Attorney General Warren: Then we have the Japanese school system here. There is no way that we know of of determining that fact.

I had together about 10 days ago about 40 district attorneys and about 40 sheriffs in the State to discuss this alien problem. I asked all of them collectively at that time if in their experience any Japanese, whether California-born or Japan-born, had ever given them any information on subversive activities or any disloyalty to this country. The answer was unanimously that no such information had ever been given to them.

Now, that is almost unbelievable. You see, when we deal with the German aliens, when we deal with the Italian aliens, we have many informants who are most anxious to help the local authorities and the State and Federal authorities to solve this alien problem. They come in voluntarily and give us information. We get none from the other source.

Does that answer your question, Congressman?

Mr. Arnold: That answers it fully.

Vigilantism

Attorney General Warren: There is one thing that concerns us at the present time. As I say, we are very happy over the order of the President yesterday. We believe that is the thing that should be done, but that is only one-half of the problem, as we see it. It is one thing to take these people out of the area and it is another thing to do something with them after they get out. Even from the small areas that they have left up to the present time there are many, many Japanese who are now roaming around the State and roaming around the Western States in a condition that will unquestionably bring about race riots and prejudice and hysteria, and excesses of all kind.

I hate to say it, but we have had some evidence of it in our State in just the last 2 or 3 days. People do not want these Japanese just loaded from one community to another, and as a practical matter it might be a very bad thing to do because we might just be transposing the danger from one place to another.

So it seems to me that the next thing the Government has to do is to find a way of handling these aliens who are removed from any vital zone.

In the county of Tulare at the present time and in the county of San Benito and in other counties there are large numbers of the Japanese moving in and sometimes the suggestion has come from the place that they leave, that they ought to go to this other community. But when they go there they find a hostile situation. We are very much afraid that it will cause trouble unless there is a very prompt solution of this problem.

My own belief concerning vigilantism is that the people do not engage in vigilante activities so long as they believe that their Government through its agencies is taking care of their most serious problem. But when they get the idea that their problems are not understood, when their Government is not doing for them the things that they believe should be done, they start taking the law into their own hands.

That is one reason why we are so happy that this committee is out here today because we believe that it will help us solve this problem quickly, which is just as important as to solve it permanently. . . .

Japanese Land Ownership

Now, gentlemen, I have some maps which show the character of the Japanese land ownership and possessory interests in California. I will submit them at the time I submit a formal statement on the subject. These maps show to the law enforcement officers that it is more than just accident, that many of those ownerships are located where they are. We base that assumption not only upon the fact that they are located in certain places, but also on the time when the ownership was acquired.

It seems strange to us that airplane manufacturing plants should be entirely surrounded by Japanese land occupancies. It seems to us that it is more than circumstance that after certain Government air bases were established Japanese undertook farming operations in close proximity to them. You can hardly grow a jackrabbit in some of the places where they presume to be carrying on farming operations close to an Army bombing base.

Many of our vital facilities, and most of our highways are just pocketed by Japanese ownerships that could be of untold danger to us in time of stress.

So we believe, gentlemen, that it would be wise for the military to take every protective measure that it believes is necessary to protect this State and this Nation against the possible activities of these people.

The Danger of American-Born Japanese

C.B. Horrall

> The following essay is excerpted from a letter sent by Los
> Angeles police chief C.B. Horrall to California attorney
> general Earl Warren on February 19, 1942. Horrall argues
> that the greatest threat to the security of the Los Angeles area
> comes from the American-born children of Japanese immi-
> grants. According to Horrall, the majority of these Japanese
> Americans received the greater part of their education in
> Japan, where they were indoctrinated with Japanese militarist
> propaganda. Since they were born and raised in the United
> States, and are well versed in its language and customs, they
> freely associate and mingle in all areas of American life. This
> makes them better suited for intelligence gathering, according
> to Horrall, and these American-born Japanese would be able
> to provide valuable assistance to any Japanese invasion force.

The enemy alien presents numerous problems to the local law enforcement agencies endeavoring to keep them
properly supervised.

Undoubtedly the most serious menaces are potential fifth-
column activities, sabotage, and espionage. To properly control these activities, it is necessary to maintain constant police patrols and a constant investigative check on the
activities of the enemy alien residing in these districts.

Reprinted from a letter of C.B. Horrall to Earl Warren dated February 19, 1942, which
was entered into Exhibit B as part of testimony before the U.S. House Select Committee
Investigating National Defense Migration, Washington, D.C., February 21, 23, 1942.

The situation in the Los Angeles area is probably more acute than in any other district, due to the fact that there are approximately 25,000 Japanese within a 5-minute walking distance of our city hall, county hall of justice, hall of records, and the Federal and State buildings. This number, plus an additional five or six thousand, are also within a very short driving distance of our numerous aviation plants and other defense projects, and numerous army encampments which are usually in close proximity to a major defense plant.

Sabotage of the Aviation Industry

The aviation industry presents the gravest situation because this area represents approximately 50 percent of the aviation production of the entire United States. While the sabotage possibilities are fairly well controlled with the protection now afforded, it is an utter impossibility to completely control espionage activities because the information as to production rates, types, and models of planes produced can be readily ascertained from the scrutinizing or photographing of the planes while on the testing fields of these plants, by possible espionage agents living or residing within a reasonable radius.

The method of handling these types of activities is that of additional police personnel being assigned to patrol and investigate units in these suspected areas. With the limited personnel that this department has at the present time, the release of sufficient officers from other required duties to properly supervise this is impossible. In addition to the fire-prevention activities, there is also the increased service of investigating suspects and patrolling and policing of major public utilities.

One condition which creates a hazard is the fact that near the beaches we have large open areas which are utilized by Japanese truck farmers. This is a very fertile field for short-wave receiving and sending sets, as well as signaling devices. A specific instance of this presented itself here on December 8 and 9, wherein a large amount of loose hay was piled in the shape of an arrow pointing to one of our major aviation plants. This was presumably done with the intention of directing aerial activities toward this location.

Due to the complex problems presented in handling this enemy alien situation, I believe that all enemy aliens should be removed from the coastal areas for a distance of 250 to 300 miles, and be supervised in such a manner that they be continually under surveillance of responsible authorities.

The Danger of American-Born Japanese

It is my opinion that your teletype request overlooked one of our most hazardous situations, which is that of the American-born Japanese. After a thorough and complete investigation of the relationship existing between parents and

Resolution 22113

Following are excerpts from Resolution 22113, adopted by the Portland City Council on February 19, 1942. The resolution calls for the removal and internment of all West Coast residents of Japanese ancestry for the duration of the war.

Whereas a state of war exists between the Government of the United States and the Government of Japan and it is of paramount importance to the people of this Nation that the possibilities for fifth-column activities be reduced to a minimum; and

Whereas there are on the Pacific coast of the United States many Japanese nationals and persons of Japanese descent irrespective of American citizenship, including many residents of the State of Oregon, who, under the existing circumstances, should be subject to restrictions by the United States in order that possible fifth-column activities be minimized; and

Whereas it may be true that many such Japanese nationals and persons of Japanese descent irrespective of American citizenship are not in accord with the aggression practiced by the Japanese Government, the public welfare demands that the paramount importance of the safety of this children, and the tendencies of the American-born Japanese, I feel that they present as difficult, if not a more difficult, problem than the enemy alien. They are cognizant of the American custom of living; they are capable of understanding the American language and inference; and, subject to small limitations, are allowed to associate and mingle with the general American public.

It is a well-known Japanese family tradition that the father of the family is the dominating and guiding factor for the formulating of ideas in his children and there is no doubt that the American-born Japanese is, to a great extent, imbued with the same ideas of his parents. In addition to the family traits and the patriotism for the native country of Japan, you

---

Nation subjugates such individual attitude on the part of individual Japanese nationals and persons of Japanese descent irrespective of American citizenship, residents of this country, inasmuch as it is impossible to determine by any known process the actual loyalty of such resident Japanese nationals and persons of Japanese descent irrespective of American citizenship; and

Whereas the report of the special commission appointed by the President to investigate circumstances incident to the attack on Pearl Harbor on December 7, 1941, clearly indicates the extent to which fifth-column activities had been operating in the islands of the Hawaiian group: Now, therefore, be it

Resolved. That the council of the city of Portland in regular session assembled does by this resolution memorialize the Government of the United States through its respective agencies and departments to take appropriate steps immediately to intern and remove from the coastal areas of the United States all Japanese nationals and persons of Japanese descent irrespective of American citizenship, that the same be interned for the duration of the war and thus kept under proper supervision by the Government of this Nation.

Reprinted from evidence submitted to the U.S. House Select Committee Investigating National Defense Migration, Washington, D.C., February 21, 23, and March 2, 1942.

have racial characteristics, that of being a Mongolian, which cannot be obliterated from these persons, regardless of how many generations are born in the United States.

You have, also, one other problem, that of about 40 percent of American-born Japanese having returned, either voluntarily, or at the request of their parents, to Japan, and having received the greater portion of their education in that country. A large number of these Ki-bei have even attended military schools in Japan and the fathers of a considerable number of them have received decorations for military bravery or military administrative work while residing in this country, either prior to, or since, the Ki-bei returned from Japan.

Questionable Loyalty

Our officers personally interviewed a large number of the American-born Japanese and while some of them staunchly maintained their patriotism to the United States, they all stated that if Japan should be victorious in this war they would have a certain amount of pride for the accomplishment of that country.

It is my opinion that the danger, especially for fifth-column activities in this district, is serious. This is due to the fact that there are some twenty-five to thirty thousand Japanese in this area and the location of a large portion of these are in very strategic areas. These strategic areas are in the very close proximity of the coastal regions where an invasion party would necessarily be landed. I have no doubt that they would lend any and all assistance possible to a Japanese land invasion, and several of the Japanese who are believed to be as patriotic as any, have expressed the above opinion in interviews.

Another situation presents itself in that the areas described above have full and complete view of all navigation in and out of our local harbor and have constant scrutiny of the activities maintained in the harbor districts. Some incidents have happened in our harbor district which lends very strongly to the opinion that espionage information is being, or has been, disseminated from that area.

Italian and German Aliens

As to the Italian and German aliens, I feel that they present a lesser menace than the Japanese, due to the fact that we are fortunate in having a smaller number in our midst. However, the number is somewhat offset by the intelligence and viciousness of the German alien. It is a well-known fact that German aliens, before being permitted to come into this country by the German Government, were required to leave some of their immediate relatives or family in Germany, and that they were allowed to come into this country for one specific purpose only, and that was to develop and return certain information to the German Secret Service. If this information is not forwarded, the positive instructions are left with these individuals that their family and friends left in Germany will be mistreated or placed in concentration camps.

This same policy is maintained as to several of the countries which have fallen under German domination since the beginning of the war. To realize the seriousness of this situ-

Fear of sabotage and espionage by American-born Japanese led many to distrust their neighbors.

ation, you should consider the Army and Navy activities, etc., in this area and the number of manufacturing plants of defense implements which are readily accessible for sabotage and espionage purpose.

I can see no reason to differentiate between different types of aliens. In my opinion there is only one procedure to follow in handling this situation, which is the concentration of each and every one of the three classes of enemy aliens and I do not feel that any material difference exists in their potential danger to the internal security of this country.

Japanese Aliens Pose a Greater Threat than German and Italian Aliens

Angelo J. Rossi

Japanese aliens represent more of a danger to the security of
Pacific coast communities than aliens of German and Italian
descent, argues San Francisco mayor Angelo J. Rossi. Citing
proof of Japanese American sabotage at Pearl Harbor and the
threat of similar sabotage on the Pacific shore, Rossi contends
that Japanese residents should be removed from the West
Coast. However, Rossi explains, residents of Italian and German descent should not be removed as their removal would
disrupt their lives and the community. Moreover, Rossi argues,
American citizens of Japanese descent should be subjected to
a rigorous test of their loyalty to the United States. The following essay is excerpted from Rossi's testimony before the
Tolan Committee hearings on National Defense Migration.

I am of the belief that the seriousness of having alien enemies in our midst is self-evident. Their presence might
not only affect the property of our citizenry and our Government but it might also affect the very lives and welfare
of all of our people. The problem is a most difficult one, but
we are living in times when a delicate problem must be
firmly dealt with. It is true that the recent drastic measures

Excerpted from Angelo J. Rossi's testimony before the U.S. House Select Committee Investigating National Defense Migration, Washington, D.C., February 21, 23, 1942.

against enemy aliens have caused great anxiety and distress among this group of people. It is true also that as a result of these measures many San Francisco families will be deprived of their livelihood. Many families will have to abandon their homes, their businesses, and their occupations; parents will have to abandon their children and go elsewhere. The great majority of noncitizens in this area is made up of elderly men and women whom I believe for the most part to be industrious, peaceful and law-abiding residents of this community. Most of them have native-born children. Many of them have sons in the armed forces and both sons and daughters engaged in defense industries and civilian defense activities. It is the well-considered opinion of many that most of these people are entirely loyal to this Nation, are in accord with its form of Government, believe in its ideals and have an affection for its traditions and that under no circumstances would they engage in any subversive activities or conduct.

The Japanese Situation

It has been said that the measures which are proposed to be taken against these aliens, instead of making for national solidarity and unity of effort in this emergency may cause dissatisfaction and resentment among those of alien parentage. In my opinion all of the above-mentioned elements should be given serious consideration before any more drastic measures are taken. In my opinion the above-mentioned facts apply particularly to the German and Italian alien problems. Their problems should be considered separately from those of the Japanese.

The Japanese situation should be given immediate attention. It admits of no delay. The activities of the Japanese saboteurs and fifth columnists in Honolulu and on the battle fronts in the Pacific have forced me to the conclusion that every Japanese alien should be removed from this community. I am also strongly of the conviction that Japanese who are American citizens should be subjected to a more detailed and all-encompassing investigation. After investigation, if it is found that these citizens are not loyal to this country they, too, should be removed from the community.

The general statements I made at the outset, I repeat, pertain mainly to persons of German and Italian origin, many of whom are engaged in business, occupations pursued by them for years, the character of some of which necessarily enters into the welfare of San Francisco. The great majority of these aliens likewise have children, most of whom were born, reared, and educated in this community and are law-abiding citizens.

German and Italian Aliens Should Not Be Moved

It must be obvious that if these alien residents about whom I have just made mention are moved from San Francisco, separated from their children and families, and deprived of the occupations in which they are now and for years have been engaged, they will be subjected to extreme hardship, mental distress, and suffering.

My opinion is that such results should be avoided, and that evacuation of Axis aliens, other than Japanese, should be avoided unless deemed imperative. If immediate removal is deemed necessary, as quickly thereafter as is conveniently practical, such aliens should be permitted to make application to resume their former places of residence (other than in prohibited areas) and their present occupations and such applications should be heard by some appropriate tribunal which could quickly and intelligently determine the same, and that in the event such applicant is found to be a person of loyalty and integrity, the desired permit be issued, subject, however, to such restrictions as might be deemed necessary.

Effect on Community of Evacuation of Workers

It is my belief that what may happen to German and Italian aliens on and after February 24, 1942, as a result of their removal from this community should be given immediate consideration. I believe that some satisfactory and equitable solution of the problems that under such circumstances will arise should be immediately brought about. I refer particularly to fishermen, janitors, garbage collectors, produce and vegetable workers in markets, and the alien workers in various other fields of human activity, all of whom will have to be provided with special permits in order to enable them to carry on their occupations and engage in the conduct of their business after 9 P.M. if the ordinary commercial routine of our city is to be maintained. Aside from these manual workers there are a number of aliens engaged in the practice of their professions who likewise will be affected by the 9 P.M. regulations to which attention should be given.

In my opinion, in order to avoid injustice being done, the investigation of such individual case of German and Italian aliens is absolutely necessary.

I believe it is appropriate that I should advise this committee that we have in our community many outstanding citizens of high standing of all nationalities. These citizens are willing to cooperate in every possible way to assist the duly constituted authorities in solving the problems above mentioned and would be glad to act upon request. The Department of Morale of the Civilian Defense Council is in touch with these citizens and will gladly recommend to the proper officials their names.

I wish to urge upon this committee the necessity of executing every effort to bring about an increase in the staffs of the local Federal Bureau of Investigation, of the Department of Naturalization, and the Department of Immigration. Each of these departments is confronted with an enormous task. At the present time all these departments are understaffed. The dependency of this community upon these three organizations is enormous.

The Japanese Attempt to Colonize the West Coast

Miller Freeman

> In the following excerpts from his written statement and oral
> testimony given before the Tolan Committee Hearings on
> National Defense Migration, publisher Miller Freeman argues
> that Japanese immigration to America was an attempt by the
> Japanese government to colonize the West Coast of the United
> States. In circumventing two attempts to restrict Japanese immi-
> gration to America, Freeman points out, the Japanese govern-
> ment was able to plant 300,000 of her people in the United
> States. Moreover, Freeman argues, though many residents of
> Japanese ancestry are American citizens, their loyalty to the
> United States is highly questionable because many of them were
> educated in Japan, where they were indoctrinated with Japanese
> militaristic propaganda. Also, Freeman argues, there was a con-
> spicuous lack of condemnation of Japanese aggression in South-
> east Asia by the Japanese American community. Because the
> loyalty of Japanese Americans is questionable, Freeman argues,
> their removal from the West Coast is a necessity.

It is my recommendation that all Japanese, both alien and
United States born, be evacuated from the Pacific Coast
States, and other defense areas, and kept in the interior un-
der strict control for the duration of the war.

While it may be argued that many American-born Japa-

Excerpted from Miller Freeman's testimony before the U.S. House Select Committee Investigating National Defense Migration, Washington, D.C., February 21, 23, 1942.

nese are loyal to the United States there are sufficient numbers who are proven to be assisting Japan's war effort to warrant such action, not only in the Nation's interest, but for protection of the Japanese themselves.

Two-thirds of the Japanese in this country are now American born, largely of mature years. Those who are genuinely loyal find themselves in their present difficult position through the treacherous attack by Japan on this nation, and because of their own sins of omission.

No Display of Loyalty

Although the American born are strongly organized for proclaimed patriotic purposes, why have they taken no stand against the aggressions of Japan in the Orient over the past 10 years? Why have they not denounced the depredations and enslavement by Japan of the Chinese, the Koreans and other Asiatics?

Why have the loyal American-born Japanese not forced the closing of the hundreds of Japanese-language schools that have been operated continuously right up to December 7 for nearly a half-century in the United States and Hawaii, the sole function of these schools being to train the children up to owe their allegiance to Japan?

Why also have they continued Japanese-language newspapers? Practically all, aliens and American-born alike, read English. Only after the attack by Japan on this country were the Japanese-language newspapers converted into English.

Study of the historical record of Japanese colonization in the United States and its possessions should be made by your committee. The bound volumes containing hearings held by the House Committee on Immigration and Naturalization on the Pacific coast in 1919 and 1920 will supply you with much authoritative information. Such study will show that the Japanese Government as a part of its ambitious program of colonization of North and South America, and as a preliminary to conquest, planted its immigrants in the United States by the combined use of fraud, collusion, political and military force, and over the most intense and sustained opposition of the various States of the Pacific coast, and the Territory of Hawaii.

The First Japanese Immigrants

The first Japanese immigrants were brought into Hawaii in 1868, numbering 350, as peons, for a period of 3 years service at $4 per month under contract to sugar planters. Then years later the business had become systematized and grown to alarming proportions in the hands of Japanese emigration syndicates. Prof. W.D. Alexander, in his book *The History of the Hawaiian People,* said:

> Having ascertained that extensive frauds were being practiced on these people, and that the immigration laws were being evaded, the Hawaiian Government caused a strict examination to be made, and on the 23d of March 1897, forbade the landing of several hundred Japanese immigrants. In all, about 1,100 immigrants on different occasions were obliged to return to Japan, where this severe action excited intense feeling. The Japanese Government sent the cruiser *Naniwa* in May, with a special commissioner, to investigate the matter. After a lengthy correspondence, the difficulty was amicably compromised the next year by the payment of an indemnity of $75,000 to Japan. This was done at the instance of the United States Government, to remove a possible hindrance to annexation.

It is thus seen that as early as 1896 the attempt was made by the Hawaiian Government to avert being inundated by the Japanese hordes, but they were compelled to yield to force, combined with pressure by the United States Government, and Hawaii was required to pay a considerable sum by way of damages for its resistance.

The Gentlemen's Agreement

In 1907 the rising tide of public sentiment on the Pacific coast against the unrestricted immigration by Japanese syndicates crystallized in a demand for exclusion. In his biography Theodore Roosevelt relates how he was told by Japan that if Congress passed such an act she would declare war; that he was genuinely alarmed because Japan had a great army of veterans trained in wars with China and Russia, and that he therefore accepted Japan's proposal to enter into the so-called gentlemen's agreement, by which Japan agreed on her honor to keep her nationals out of the country. That agreement was generally accepted as a happy solution of the problem. . . .

In the decade between 1910 and 1920 the Japanese population in the United States and Hawaii increased by 68,452.

Between 1920 and 1930 the Japanese population increased by 58,181.

In the 1930–40 decade it increased by 6,387. However, the Japanese population in the United States during this period decreased by 11,887. When the births in the continental United States are figured in for this decade this would mean a total decrease of at least 25,000. Where did those people go? How many additional have left since 1940? If

The Governor of Colorado Supports Relocation

Following are excerpts from a February 28, 1942, radio address given by Colorado governor Ralph L. Carr. In the address, Governor Carr asserts the importance of preventing fifth-column activities by enemy aliens and pledges Colorado's support in any relocation program.

There can be no question that the attacks on Pearl Harbor and the Philippines were aided by fifth columnists. The potency of that evil organization has been proved in every European country which has fallen, exemplified by the desertion of France, as Winston Churchill described it, and the rape of Norway and the rest. The overthrow of any nation is assured when the approach of an attacking force is made smooth and paved by subversive activities within.

Along the Pacific coast there are thousands of persons who are not friendly to those things which we call American. The wire for the survey suggests that they are Germans, [those Japanese went] to Japan to enter the service of that country against the United States, will they be welcomed back with open arms at the end of the war?

In the same decade Japanese population in Hawaii increased by 18,274. Where did this increase come from? The increase in Hawaii would have been nearer 30,000 for the 1930–40 decade except for emigration to Japan or the mainland.

Your committee should obtain the answers to these questions for the future guidance of the Federal Government.

Deception

Japan has accomplished the miraculous feat of permanently planting 300,000 of her people in this country, quadrupling it since the gentlemen's agreement was entered into in 1907. Compound this population's birth rate over the next 50 years

---

Italians, and Japanese. Only Monday night of this week the beautiful country surrounding Santa Barbara in southern California was attacked by an enemy submarine which came to the surface and hurled shells at a great supply of gasoline. The enemy has become so confident that he knocks at the very front door of one of the great cities of the world and attacks the mainland of the United States. . . .

If those who command the armed forces of our Nation say that it is necessary to remove any persons from the Pacific coast and call upon Colorado to do her part in this war by furnishing temporary quarters for those individuals, we stand ready to carry out that order. If any enemy aliens must be transferred as a war measure, then we of Colorado are big enough and patriotic enough to do our duty. We announce to the world that 1,118,000 red-blooded citizens of this State are able to take care of 3,500 or any number of enemies, if that be the task which is allotted to us.

Exhibit 19—Text of a Radio Address given by Hon. Ralph L. Carr, Governor of Colorado, on February 28, 1942, *National Defense Migration: Hearings on H.R. 113*, 77th Congress, Second Session February 26 and 28, and March 2, 1942.

and it becomes clear that we are handing on to future generations a problem of an insoluble race that will continue to become increasingly grave. This could only have been accomplished by the weakness of the National Government in failing to resist Japan's colonization efforts and enforce the principles and the spirit of the exclusion measures that had been adopted. We were deceived twice into thinking Japanese immigration stopped—once in 1907 and again in 1942.

Japan's designs in colonizing the Pacific Coast States and Hawaii and her ambitious plans for conquest have been abetted by pro-Japanese elements in this country, including such organizations as the Japan Society, which is national in character with local chapters in various parts of the country. The membership of the Japan Society is made up of persons employed by Japanese interests, such as lawyers and other agents, representatives of transportation companies, import and export concerns, ministers, educators, peace advocates, and represents a cross-section of public men in the communities where it operates. Some have been decorated by the Japanese Emperor for services rendered. It has had prominent officials of the United States Government as directors and members.

Economic and Political Aid to Japan

By economic and political pressure these people have been of powerful help to Japan. Only 2 years ago Japan undertook a drive to prevent abrogation of our trade treaty, which automatically stopped shipments of war materials to that country. This campaign was conducted through the Japanese Embassy and the local Japanese consuls. They lined up the people with whom they had business or other connections and got them to oppose such abrogation.

If, as believed, this is a fifth-column organization, it should be disbanded, even though the majority of the members of such organization are not consciously disloyal to America. They have simply been made suckers out of.

The day of subjugation and exploitation of defenseless millions throughout the world is about over.

The Japanese in this country now find themselves victims of an obsolete system that Japan's military government is belatedly attempting to enforce on the world.

American-born Japanese have a very real opportunity to participate in the establishment of an era that is now dawning, of equal rights, freedom and justice to all, regardless of race. They should utilize the education they have gained in this democracy and openly adopt a program dedicating themselves to the accomplishment of this purpose, thus contributing materially to the permanent peace and security of the peoples of all the world.

Oral Testimony

Mr. Curtis [Rep. Carl T. Curtis]: . . . What recommendations would you make as to where aliens should be moved, if they are moved?

Mr. Freeman: Into the interior.

Mr. Curtis: What do you mean by the interior?

Mr. Freeman: Off the coast, or away from any defense areas.

Mr. Curtis: Do you mean the center of the United States, or do you mean just back from the coast?

Mr. Freeman: I would say anywhere where they would be away from military activities or any danger of harming the defense activities of industries in this country. There are plenty of areas it seems to me in which you could put them. I think the offer of Governor Carr [of Colorado], for instance, is well worth considering. [Carr offered to resettle Japanese Americans in Colorado.]

Mr. Curtis: What distinction, if any, would you make between alien Japanese and citizen Japanese?

Mr. Freeman: None.

Mr. Curtis: You would move everybody?

Mr. Freeman: Yes. I would like to elaborate on that, and briefly give my reasons why.

Mr. Curtis: Yes.

Mr. Freeman: I will try to brief this down. To begin with, immigration started in this country in the very early days, first in Hawaii. The Kingdom of Hawaii objected strenuously to the infiltration of Japanese. It finally refused to permit them to land, and in 1879, the Government of Hawaii, having rejected the Japanese, the Government of Japan sent a warship to Hawaii and made them take them, and also made them pay indemnity of $75,000. And, by the way, that was done on the urgent requests of the United States Government, which was at that time preparing to annex this country. Immigration began in the United States proper, in the early 1900's. By 1906 and 1907 it became alarming. Theodore Roosevelt undertook negotiations with Japan. The sentiment on the Pacific coast was rising. They finally entered into what was known as a gentlemen's agreement. That was in 1907. Between the time that that deal was entered into and the negotiations————

Mr. Curtis: Well, now, Mr. Freeman, in your written statement we will be very happy to have this historical background, but I wish you would tell me briefly why you feel that any evacuation order should cover citizen Japanese as well as alien Japanese.

Mr. Freeman: Well, I will tell you right now that I will not be but a minute.

Mr. Curtis: All right.

Mr. Freeman: Theodore Roosevelt agreed to enter into a gentlemen's agreement on the proposal offered by Japan. That agreement was negotiated in 1907; but between the time it was negotiated and before the act was put into effect, 30,000 more Japanese were put into this country by the Japanese Government. All this infiltration was by syndicates, semiofficial, and financed and operated out of Japan, and for one purpose only, and that was colonizing the Pacific coast.

I claim that they are here by fraud, deception, and collusion, and with the assistance of what we might call fifth-column organizations, such as the Japan Society. By the way, I want to suggest that you gentlemen take a little longer view than merely coming here and holding these hearings, but get at some of the underlying factors as to why this condition exists today.

Indoctrination in Japanese Language Schools

All this time the Japanese who are here have been trained in Japanese language schools. Their doctrine has been controlled through the Japanese Government, and by teachers who are assigned for one purpose only, and that is to teach and train these people up in loyalty to Japan, and that is the reason you have them indoctrinated today, and that is the reason why they are dangerous.

It is a very remarkable fact that these language schools have been conducted by the hundreds in this country and in Hawaii, and that the United States Government has allowed it, and the State governments have permitted it to be done without supervision.

The fact is, however, that they are here, and that they have been trained up, not in the ways of Americans, but that their education has been primarily to maintain their loyalty to Japan.

I don't say at all that a lot of these Japanese are not loyal citizens; but I say that there is a high percentage who are not loyal, and that you will have the evidence to show that that is true.

Mr. Curtis: Now, at that point, let me draw a distinction between, perhaps, the method of handling the Italians and Germans and the Japanese.

Mr. Freeman: Well, I am not qualified to say what should be done about the Germans and Italians. I would say that any alien who has been here for any length of time and who has not taken advantage of the very generous and liberal opportunity to become a citizen, is at least a suspect.

I just want to add one point more, and that is that the Japanese who have been in this country for many years and have enjoyed these benefits—I have never seen, and I don't think that there has been any evidence to show, that they have objected individually or in an organized way to the aggressions by the Japanese Government in China or in Asia. They are educated here, and certainly if they have the ideals of a democracy, of the United States, what they could do would be of tremendous value.

One instance only I will give you. It happened only the last 2 years of the drive by the Japanese Government to prevent the abrogation of the trade treaty. That trade treaty was permitting large amounts of scrap iron and war materials to go into Japan. The drive was undertaken here, and it was through the office of the Japanese consul and Mitsubishi & Co., and supported by some of our more representative citizens who have business relations with them. The Japanese are able to apply organized pressure and are very successful in their efforts, and have been from the very earliest date. They have been highly organized, and the white man hasn't. It has included the employment of men who are high in public office, including such men as former Attorney General Wickersham, who was the Attorney General in the Taft Administration, and who afterward became the attorney for large Japanese interests; and he was the man that defended Mitsui & Co., who had operated two airplane plants in the United States, and as shown by the Committee of Investigation after the war, got millions of dollars from the United States Government. They were indicted, but nothing ever happened about it.

Mr. Curtis: I want to ask you one more question.

Mr. Freeman: All right.

Mr. Curtis: What work, if any, could these people be put to that would help to contribute to our war production and our civilian needs, in the event they are moved?

Mr. Freeman: First of all, they ought to be taken out of this coast country. What should be done with them after we get them back there, whether they are put into employment—if it is possible to find it, certainly I would do it. If it isn't, however, I certainly would still remove them from this area.

Mr. Curtis: I want to thank you for your coming in, and any further statement that you wish to make———

Mr. Freeman (interposing): I have made a written statement, but I would be glad to have you ask any further questions. However, I will say this, just once more, and that is that we have year after year these investigations, including the congressional committees that come out here, and the trouble is that they deal with our problems only in a super-ficial way. I would like to see you extend your investigations to the underlying factors. You have spoken of Pearl Harbor. Now, I would suggest that you look into influences, such as the fifth-column organizations, and whether you do it your-selves or whether you recommend it be undertaken by oth-er Federal agencies I think that it should be done.

Mr. Curtis: We agree with you.

Mr. Bender [Rep. George H. Bender]: Mr. Freeman, let me ask you just one question.

Mr. Freeman: Yes.

Mr. Bender: You stated that you thought the Japanese should become better citizens, and at the same time you said that for years you have advocated exclusion. How can they become better citizens when this country won't let them be-come better citizens?

Mr. Freeman: No; I don't think that question is correct. I think that every opportunity has been given, most gener-ously, in education and opportunities. These people have had the utmost freedom and opportunities to engage in business activities of every sort. As a matter of fact, the whole trend of this thing in immigration and in the ways in which they are tied up with Japan show that their interests have been much more with Japan than with this country.

Japanese Immigration

Between 1910 and 1920, Japan entered into this so-called gentlemen's agreement by which Japan agreed on her honor to stay out of this country. Sixty-eight thousand more of them came in. Between 1920 and 1930, we had nearly 60,000 more, and they came in under the so-called Exclusion Act.

You have other factors about the immigration question that I think should be looked into. During the last 10 years, there has been withdrawn from this country some thousands of Japanese. Where did they go? If they went back to Japan to enter the armed forces of the country, after the war is over, are we going to welcome them back with open arms?

Chapter 2

The Internment of the Issei

Chapter Preface

While the majority of Japanese evacuees from the West Coast were interned in relocation camps administered by the War Relocation Authority (WRA), certain Issei (first generation Japanese immigrants), along with some individuals of German and Italian descent, were incarcerated in camps operated by the Department of Justice. These inmates—classified as "dangerous enemy aliens"—were generally older men who were suspected by the FBI of having ties with the government of Japan. Some were diplomats, and the majority of them were leaders in the Japanese community who were rounded up in the days immediately following the attack on Pearl Harbor.

On numerous occasions Japanese American children came home from school to find the FBI searching their homes and taking their fathers away. Families sometimes went weeks without being able to communicate with loved ones that were taken into custody. Barry Saiki's father had initially been spared separation from his family because of a physical ailment. As the Saiki family prepared for their evacuation from Stockton, California, however, two FBI agents approached them and Saiki's father was taken away. "In ten minutes they were gone," Saiki recalls. "It was to be almost a year before we learned of his whereabouts—the Lordsburg Internment Camp in New Mexico."

Although inmates at the Justice Department camps were kept under high security, they lived similarly to the evacuees in WRA camps. They lived in barracks-style housing and were allowed to develop recreation, education, and work programs. Women and children were eventually allowed to join their husbands and fathers at one Justice Department camp in Crystal City, Texas. The majority of inmates, however, remained separated from their families for the duration of the war, able to communicate only through censored letters.

The Night the FBI Came for My Father

Yoshiko Uchida

In the following essay, Yoshiko Uchida, a resident of Berkeley, California at the outbreak of World War II, writes of her
family's experience in the wake of the Japanese attack on
Pearl Harbor. Upon her return home from the school library
that day, Uchida discovered that FBI agents had taken her
father, along with virtually every leader of the Japanese community, into custody. Six days would pass before Uchida's
family received word from her father. He had been taken to
the Immigration Detention Quarters in San Francisco, and
was soon to be transferred to a camp for enemy aliens in Missoula, Montana. Uchida writes of her family's struggle to
conduct business affairs in the absence of her father, who was
only allowed to communicate with his wife and daughters
through censored letters. The following essay is excerpted
from Uchida's memoir, *Desert Exile: The Uprooting of a Japanese American Family*.

It was one of those rare Sundays when we had no guests
for dinner. My parents, sister, and I had just come home
from church and were having a quiet lunch when we heard
a frenzied voice on the radio break in on the program. The
Japanese had attacked Pearl Harbor.

"Oh no," Mama cried out. "It can't be true."

"Of course not," Papa reassured her. "And if it is, it's only
the work of a fanatic."

We all agreed with him. Of course it could only be an aberrant act of some crazy irresponsible fool. It never for a moment occurred to any of us that this meant war. As a matter of fact, I was more concerned about my approaching finals at the university than I was with this bizarre news and went to the library to study. When I got there, I found clusters of Nisei [second generation Japanese American] students anxiously discussing the shocking event. But we all agreed it was only a freak incident and turned our attention to our books. I stayed at the library until 5:00 P.M. giving no further thought to the attack on Pearl Harbor.

Japanese Community Leaders Are Seized

When I got home, the house was filled with an uneasy quiet. A strange man sat in our living room and my father was gone. The FBI had come to pick him up, as they had dozens of other Japanese men. Executives of Japanese business firms, shipping lines, and banks, men active in local Japanese associations, teachers of Japanese language schools, virtually every leader of the Japanese American community along the West Coast had been seized almost immediately.

Actually the FBI had come to our house twice, once in the absence of my parents and sister who, still not realizing the serious nature of the attack, had gone out to visit friends. Their absence, I suppose, had been cause for suspicion and the FBI or police had broken in to search our house without a warrant. On returning, my father, believing that we had been burglarized, immediately called the police. Two policemen appeared promptly with three FBI men and suggested that my father check to see if his valuables were missing. They were, of course, undisturbed, but their location was thereby revealed. Two of the FBI men requested that my father accompany them "for a short while" to be questioned, and my father went willingly. The other FBI man remained with my mother and sister to intercept all phone calls and to inform anyone who called that they were indisposed.

One policeman stationed himself at the front door and the other at the rear. When two of our white friends came to see how we were, they were not permitted to enter or speak to my mother and sister, who, for all practical purposes, were prisoners in our home.

Fear

By the time I came home, only one FBI man remained but I was alarmed at the startling turn of events during my absence. In spite of her own anxiety, Mama in her usual thoughtful way was serving tea to the FBI agent. He tried to be friendly and courteous, reassuring me that my father would return safely in due time. But I couldn't share my mother's gracious attitude toward him. Papa was gone, and his abrupt custody into the hands of the FBI seemed an ominous portent of worse things to come. I had no inclination to have tea with one of its agents, and went abruptly to my room, slamming the door shut.

Eventually, after a call from headquarters, the FBI agent left, and Mama, Kay, and I were alone at last. Mama made supper and we sat down to eat, but no one was hungry. Without Papa things just weren't the same, and none of us dared voice the fear that sat like a heavy black stone inside each of us.

"Let's leave the porch light on and the screen door unlatched," Mama said hopefully. "Maybe Papa will be back later tonight."

But the next morning the light was still burning, and we had no idea of his whereabouts. All that day and for three days that followed, we had no knowledge of what had happened to my father. And somehow during those days, I struggled through my finals.

Word from San Francisco

It wasn't until the morning of the fifth day that one of the men apprehended with my father, but released because he was an American citizen, called to tell us that my father was being detained with about one hundred other Japanese men at the Immigration Detention Quarters in San Francisco. The following day a postcard arrived from Papa telling us where he was and asking us to send him his shaving kit and some clean clothes. "Don't worry, I'm all right," he wrote, but all we knew for certain was that he was alive and still in San Francisco.

As soon as permission was granted, we went to visit him at the Immigration Detention Quarters, a drab, dreary institutional structure. We went in, anxious and apprehensive, and were told to wait in a small room while my father was summoned from another part of the building. As I stepped to the door and looked down the dingy hallway, I saw Papa coming toward me with a uniformed guard following close behind. His steps were eager, but he looked worn and tired.

"Papa! Are you all right?"

He hugged each of us.

"I'm all right. I'm fine," he reassured us.

The Joy Is Short-Lived

But our joy in seeing him was short-lived, for he told us that he was among a group of ninety men who would be transferred soon to an army internment camp in Missoula, Montana.

"Montana!" we exclaimed. "But we won't be able to see you anymore then."

"I know," Papa said, "but you can write me letters and I'll write you too. Write often, and be very careful—all of you. Kay and Yo, you girls take good care of Mama." His concern was more for us than for himself.

When it was time to say goodbye, none of us could speak for the ache in our hearts. My sister and I began to cry. And it was Mama who was the strong one.

The three of us watched Papa go down the dark hallway with the guard and disappear around a corner. He was gone, and we didn't know if we would ever see him again. There were rumors that men such as my father were to be held as hostages in reprisal for atrocities committed by the Japanese soldiers. If the Japanese killed American prisoners, it was possible my father might be among those killed in reprisal.

It was the first time in our lives that Papa had been separated from us against his will. We returned home in silent gloom, my sister dabbing at her eyes and blowing her nose as she drove us back to Berkeley. When we got home, we comforted ourselves by immediately packing and shipping a carton of warm clothing to Papa in Montana, glad for the opportunity to do something to help him.

As soon as our friends heard that my father had been interned, they gathered around to give us support and comfort, and for several days running we had over fifteen callers a day.

Instructions from Montana

Upon reaching Montana, my father wrote immediately, his major concern being whether we would have enough money for our daily needs. He and my mother were now classified as "enemy aliens" and his bank account had been blocked immediately. For weeks there was total confusion regarding the amount that could be withdrawn from such blocked accounts for living expenses, and early reports indicated it would be only $100 a month.

"Withdraw as much as you can from my account," Papa wrote to us. "I don't want you girls to dip into your own savings accounts unless absolutely necessary."

As the oldest citizen of our household, my sister now had to assume responsibility for managing our business affairs, and it was not an easy task. There were many important papers and documents we needed, but the FBI had confiscated all of my father's keys, including those to his safe deposit box, and their inaccessibility was a problem for us.

We exchanged a flurry of letters as my father tried to send detailed instructions on how to endorse checks on his behalf; how to withdraw money from his accounts; when and how to pay the premiums on his car and life insurance policies; what to do about filing his income tax returns which he could not prepare without his records; and later, when funds were available, how to purchase defense bonds for him. Another time he asked us to send him a check for a fellow internee who needed a loan.

Overwhelming Confusion

My father had always managed the business affairs of our household, and my mother, sister, and I were totally unprepared to cope with such tasks. Our confusion and bewilderment were overwhelming, and we could sense my father's frustration and anguish at being unable to help us except through censored letters, and later through internee telegrams which were permitted to discourage letter-writing. Papa's letters were always in English, not only for the benefit of the censor, but for my sister and me. And we could tell from each one that he was carefully reviewing in his mind every aspect of our lives in Berkeley.

"Don't forget to lubricate the car," he would write. "And be sure to prune the roses in January. Brush Laddie every day and give him a pat for me. Don't forget to send a monthly check to Grandma and take my Christmas offering to church."

In every letter he reassured us about his health, sent greetings to his friends, and expressed concern about members of our church.

"Tell those friends at church whose businesses have been closed not to be discouraged," he wrote in one of his first letters. "Tell them things will get better before long."

And he asked often about his garden.

From the early days of my father's detention, there had been talk of a review board that would hold hearings to determine whether and when each man would be released. Although Papa's letters were never discouraging in other respects, he cautioned us not to be optimistic whenever he wrote of the hearings. We all assumed it would be a long, slow process that might require months or even years.

The Board of Review

It developed that hearings for each of the interned men were to be conducted by a Board of Review comprised of the district attorney, representatives of the FBI, and immigration authorities of the area in which the men had formerly resided. The recommendation of the review board plus papers and affidavits of support were to be sent to Washington for a final decision by the attorney general. As soon as we learned of this procedure, we asked several of our white friends to send affidavits verifying my father's loyalty to the United States and supporting his early release. They all responded immediately, eager to do anything they could to help him.

The interned men did not dare hope for early release, but they were anxious to have the hearings over with. As they were called in for their interviews, some were photographed full-face only, while others were photographed in profile as well, and it was immediately rumored that those photographed twice would be detained as hostages. Two of the questions they were asked at the interview were, "Which country do you think will win the war?" and "If you had a gun in your hands, at whom would you shoot, the Americans or the Japanese?" In reply to the second question, most answered they would have to shoot straight up.

In accordance with Army policy, the men were never informed of plans in advance and were moved before they became too familiar with one installation. One morning half the men in my father's barrack were summoned, told that they were being shipped to another camp, and stripped of everything but the clothes on their backs. They were then loaded onto buses, with only a few minutes to say goodbye to their friends. Their destination was unknown.

Fortunately, my father was one of those who remained behind. He was also one of those who had been photographed only once, and at the time this seemed to him a faint but hopeful sign of eventual release.

My First Night in Jail

Yamato Ichihashi

On August 22, 1942, three months after respected Stanford
University professor Yamato Ichihashi was forced to leave his
home and his livelihood for the Japanese assembly center at
the Santa Anita racetrack outside of Los Angeles, Attorney
General Francis Biddle issued a warrant for his arrest. As a
result of past contacts with high-ranking Japanese diplomats,
Ichihashi was deemed a dangerous enemy alien who posed a
threat to the security of the United States. He was taken from
his wife Kei and sent to Sharp Park, an internment camp run
by the Immigration and Naturalization Service near San Francisco. In the following essay, adapted from Ichihashi's written
account of his detention, he describes his interrogation by
federal authorities and the conditions at Sharp Park.

*Editor's Note: This essay is transcribed with original
editor Gordon H. Chang's comments intact. Words
marked by question marks are the editor's best guess-
es regarding confusion in the original text.*

On the afternoon Saturday [August] 22, 1942, I faced an
unforgettable incident: an F.B.I. agent named Robert
Hart stationed at Red Bluff accompanied by Tule Lake Police Chief Rhodes, a local cop and Woodrow [Ichihashi's
son], came to the room at 2:30 and told me that I was "under arrest." I asked [what] was the charge and he replied no
charge as far as he knew. I was told to pack things I wanted
to take with me, but as said before, I had no spare things
with me. Hart kindly advised me to take what I had and

some money; we stopped at the Administration Building, I suppose for the purpose of clearing. After riding about 7 miles, we reached the Tule Lake jail, having stopped at a local stationery [store] to buy a copy of the August issue of "Readers' Digest" at Hart's suggestion; no other decent publications were available.

The sight of the jail shocked me; it is a concrete building about 20' x 20'; a part of the front is used as office and storeroom; the jail part was partitioned by iron-bars and walls into 2 rooms with a small hallway where [there] was a sink and toilet; each room had two simple beds. Rhodes handed me 1/2 doz. blankets, assuring me of their cleanliness. But alas the jail was smelly and dirty and full of buzzing flies. I have never seen the like in my life, and I think Hart himself shared my feelings, though in silence; and Rhodes was somewhat downcast, for the jail may be fit for the kind of humans he handles such as drunks, speed violators, lumberjacks, etc. but quite unfit for gentlemen. Here I arrived and [was] jailed at 3:30. Before Hart departed, he assured me that I would be taken out of the jail within 48 hours and so instructed Rhodes and to communicate with the San Francisco Immigration Service office, if necessary—this I learned afterward but not while in the jail. In fact, I only knew vaguely that I was [to be] taken to San Francisco, and that was all since Hart told me nothing. I asked Hart whether he was coming to remove me; and he said no, since his job had finished with the jailing; someone else was coming to transport me, and he did not tell me that a U.S. marshall had to do it.

My First Night in a Jail

Rhodes came frequently, and about 5:00 he took me to a hotel restaurant for dinner; he said that the U.S. pays for my meals and it has plenty of money and so I should eat anything I want. I had the best meals while in the jail since my evacuation. I returned to the jail, and I felt particularly the resounding noise that an iron-bar door makes; I started to think of my fate and imagined all sorts of things inevitable under the circumstances. Flies kept buzzing and mosquitoes

*A young evacuee waits with her family's belongings to be relocated to an
assembly center in 1942.*

began to visit and it was hot, smelly and disagreeable,
though Rhodes was kind enough to open all the windows
there were. Nightfall came and I tried to read and then put
out the one light in the room and tried to sleep but in vain.
The experience was so novel and the mind was in a state of
agitation; I was alone in the jail that night, but that was a
Saturday night and the nearby residents were noisy, singing
and talking loudly—a drinking party. I must have slept a few
hours toward the morning, but was up and washed at 7:00.
This my first night in a jail; what a peculiar experience!

Sunday [August 23]: Rhodes, [whom] I expected, did not
come until about 10:00. He explained that he was kept busy
till late and said sorry to make you wait for your breakfast; he
brought the Sunday "San Francisco Examiner" and refused
to take money for it, saying we have plenty of money in his
office. Then we went to the same restaurant and [ate] a hearty
breakfast. I read the paper and the magazine when I returned
to the jail; my mind strayed in every imaginable direction
since I did not know why I was in the jail. Thinking and med-

itation consumed most of the time until Rhodes appeared about 4:00 P.M. to take me for my dinner. I realized then that a jail-bird is fed only twice a day. I asked Rhodes whether I was permitted to write letters, he replied certainly; so I wrote a letter to [Stanford president Ray Lyman] Wilbur about my new experience and asked him to help. Rhodes gave me a stamp and I mailed it when Rhodes took me for a short ride about the town. That night at 12:00 a drunk was jailed and his cell was locked and he was given a bucket[?]; he sang or yelled all night, creating disturbances but without knowing what he was doing. In the morning, he was quite sober and asked me to give him some water which I did—3 cupfuls.

Waiting for the Marshall

That morning we went together to get our breakfast. The drunk was fined $10.00 Since he lost his registration (draft) card, without which he could [not find employment], Rhodes tried to get him a new one; for this purpose he wired to Fresno where he had registered. He could not get the card, but [did get] a slip explaining his status to enable him to find a job about 20 miles from Tule Lake; Rhodes suggested a place. He was freed. I was alone again. Rhodes began to worry about my removal since 48 hours expired at Monday (24th) 3:30, but the hoped for arrival of a marshall [had not materialized]. That day he spotted a U.S. marshall car and was positive that he came after me. He tried to contact him but in vain, until at midnight which he did by asking residents to help him. When he saw the marshall, the latter explained that he was here on other business (leave[?] cases in this region), but having learned of my case from Rhodes, he telephoned to the San Francisco Headquarters and was told to remove me there as soon as possible. This I was told by Rhodes on Tuesday morning [who] stated that the Marshall would come and get me in the afternoon.

We had breakfast; and about 2:00 we went for lunch and there came the marshall and his nephew from Shasta. I joined them and left for San Francisco about 3:00. We dropped off the nephew at Shasta—his home where he worked as a truck driver for Shell. We started southward and stopped at Redding for dinner; he invited me to eat all I cared. This marshall, named Hayden Saunders, an employee of the Justice Department for 20 years, proved to be very friendly and talked freely to me on all the conceivable subjects, including the war, against which he was bitterly opposed; he said about a dozen ambitious men were responsible and told me his son, Jack Saunders, a U.C. athlete (a swimmer) was killed a year ago as an aviation instructor because a defective plane had been given him; its wing fell and down he came and [was] killed. He explained the internal organization of the Justice Department; he thought the F.B.I.'s [J. Edgar] Hoover was ambitious and a self-boosting[?] politician, and as such he disliked him. . . .

The Red Bluff County Jail

Hart [had] said that I was "under arrest," but Saunders said that I was taken "into custody" since there was no charge against me.

Near Redding, Saunder's wife was born; here she and their daughter were visiting her birthplace. Hayden took me there and then decided that he himself would spend the night at the same place since he had been driving more than 17 hours that day. He took me [to] the Red Bluff Co. jail and requested its sheriff to give me the best of accommodations. The jail was a typical one, barred with a hall-way in the middle, the two sides subdivided into cells, each having 2 iron bunks double-decked and a pot unclean but with running water. I was allowed to take my bag with me, though ordinarily that is not permitted as I learned afterward. At the extreme end of the hall, there was a shower but apparently not working, and a large sink for face-washing. Of course, the interior was constructed with iron and iron bars by means of which small cells were separated from one another. There was no one else beside myself in the jail; it was quiet and cool and I slept. In the morning I was introduced to jail breakfast which [was] stuck thru a square-hole on the side of the cell; it was contained in the old-fashioned bread-baking pan—4 pieces of bread but no butter, plenty of oatmeal, 2 fried eggs and a tin-cup of coffee minus milk and sugar. This was a special treat, as I learned afterward. I ate the eggs with a piece of bread and drank coffee; then inspected the cells and I found but very few *rakugaki* [graffiti] among which a Japanese flag was found, whereas the walls of the Tule Lake jail were covered with obscene pictures and inscriptions.

About 9:30 Saunders came and [we] walked out of the jail; I was introduced to his wife and daughter and the latter's girl friend, who were all going to Sacramento where the family resides, but we went straight to San Francisco via Vallejo where I saw "balloons" of every shape floating above the navy yards as well as ships at anchor. We stopped at the San Francisco Post Office building (7th and Mission Streets) where the U.S. Attorney Frank J. Hennessy had his office (he is U.S. Attorney of the Northern District of California). We reached [there] at 2:00 P.M. Wednesday (26th), and I had a lunch at the office, opposite of which was a cage where a dozen men were locked in. The clerk in the office was a nice young man who offered me tobacco and ink to fill my pen. He smilingly said that it does not pay to be a Japanese when he fingerprinted and recorded my name and age. Saunders came out and said his boss[?] would send me back to Stanford as a result of his conversation with Hennessy, but of course I was not [so] naive as to believe it, though he might have been sincere. The school is in the military zone. He further said that he was leaving for his Sacramento home, as this office will take me to the Immigration Station Office at 801 Silver Avenue, and we parted.

The Sharp Park Detention Camp

About 3:30, 3 Germans and 3 Italians were called out of the cage and I joined them. We were put on a covered truck with an iron-net door on the back which was locked when we were in; we arrived at the Immigration Office. Here our records of name and age, etc. [were taken]; a repatriation form was signed [by others?]—no interest in my case. I was given a slip with the following items: "ICHI-HASHI, Yamato 12044/1405." This is my identification numbers, the former is the F.B.I. case, the latter is my own number. I am to be referred to as "1405." I tried to find out [as to?] why I was brought but in vain; the clerk suggested that I inquire of the Director of the Sharp Park Detention Camp whither I will be taken soon. We were then transferred to a bus and transported to the said Camp; I tried here again but in vain since the Director was absent. The following day we, the same group of 7, were returned to Silver Avenue and were photographed twice: a front view and a side view; my photo number is "#3529." In the [Sharp Park] Camp I was officially known as "1405."

I was pleasantly surprised at the make-up of this camp, particularly [after] my experience at the crowded Santa Anita Center and the spacious but monotonous Tule Lake Camp devoid of vegetation. It is situated not far from Salada Beach in a beautiful valley which is surrounded by hills covered with green trees and shrubs; on the western side between low hills the Pacific Ocean is visible. The ground is limited by tall iron net-fences and small in area; barracks 20' x 120' are well-built and painted outside and inside and are regularly arranged; there are 10 of these for [?] inmates; each accommodating about 40, divided into 5 rooms for 8 persons each; if double-decked (beds), 80 can be put in. . . .

Better Treatment

When I reached there, the flowers were in full bloom; the sight was delightful to the eye. Thus I found my sojourn there of more than 2 months strangely agreeable because of the beauty and the kindly attitude of official personnel. Beside the climate, there was either warm or cool [air?] due to fog like that of San Francisco, but never hot as in Santa Anita and Tule Lake and water is good. Consequently, I was able to keep clean and soon wore off my negro color and regained my natural complexion. Treatment was satisfactory—food abundant though often too greasy and powerfully seasoned with garlic; supplies were freely given such as toothbrush and paste, smokes, soaps, socks, underwears and lent shirts, shoes, overalls. Sheets and pillowcase were changed every Monday, blankets were clean. Here the Geneva Protocol as regards internees and prisoners of war regulates, and hence, a better treatment all around as compared with assembly and relocation centers. Graft is doubtless practiced but not to the extent done elsewhere.

For one thing, the number of detainees never exceeded 500; there are alien enemies—Japanese, German, and Italians, and "Internationals," mostly immigration cases. When I arrived there, the number was about 280, and when I left there on Oct. 26, there were only (October 21st statistics) 145 men and 22 women or 167 in all, due to release or internment. However, the increase and diminution are not indicated by the

Ichihashi Expresses His Gratitude

Following are excerpts from a letter sent by Yamato Ichihashi to Jessie Treat, the wife of Ichihashi's friend and colleague Payson Treat, after Ichihashi's release from the Sharp Park Internment Camp. In the letter, Ichihashi expresses his gratitude to the Treats for their help in obtaining his release and expresses his dismay with the inefficient bureaucracy of the federal government.

I wish to express my deep gratitude to you and Payson for what you two have done for us since our evacuation from our beloved campus and, in particular, during my sojourn, more strictly[?] my detention at the Sharp Park Camp. You made me happy in the midst of my extreme humiliation; this I shall never forget. As I now calmly review my sad experiences, I can truthfully say that they were very disagreeable but highly instructive (I learned many new things about war). I have no complaint against the American officials involved in the case, but I am still shocked about certain aspects in the procedure applied to the individuals unfortunate enough to have had similar experiences like those of mine. Consequently many suffered far more humiliating treatments, number because new arrivals came during the period. . . .

In passing, there is another similar detention camp in Southern California at Tuna Canyon where there were 17 Japanese, according to one Takahashi who was taken at Santa Anita about a month ago and then was removed from there to the Sharp Park—as he was a resident at San Francisco.

Interrogation

On September 1st, a detailed record of my life in Japan and here was registered by one Grover, an Immigration Service agent; this was apparently used as the basis of questions at the hearing, which was held on the 3rd at 3:30 P.M. at the Post Office Building. . . . An Immigration Service representative, an F.B.I. agent, a U.S. attorney and a recording

which I fortunately escaped.

You know that I have been an idealist all my life and as such I have been an admirer of American ideals. I am old enough to know better, but in the face of my recent experiences I have become more of a realist. The inefficiency and indifferences of bureaucracy everywhere shock me; in [my] case, seven weeks and five days were consumed between the hearing and the release. On October 13th I was notified of my release; I filled in a form at the official request; on the 16th I was told of the loss of that form and required a second form; that was at noon of Saturday and nothing was done about it until the following Monday. The officials needed one more week to check the truth of my "alleged" former residence at this Tule Lake project. At 3:30 o'clock P.M. (26th) I was told to pack up to be ready at 4:00; I had no time to say goodbye to a German baker who made a cake when he learned that the Japanese were holding a farewell party for me! But all this belongs to the past and I can veritably smile again; I am resettled with my family once more.

Morning Glory, Evening Shadow: Yamato Ichihashi and His Internment Writings, 1942–1945. Gordon H. Chang, ed. Stanford, CA: Stanford University Press, 1997.

secretary formed the investigation committee. Treat attended it as my witness. I was made to take an oath to tell nothing but the truth. Then [U.S.] attorney Mercado (a former
student of [Ichihashi's friend and colleague Payson] Treat
and mine) opened the hearing, and said that the President of
the United States possessed the authority to intern alien enemies without reason, adding in any case, if released, I will
be sent back to Tule Lake. The questions asked concerned
my publications, my participation in international confer-
ences diplomatic and scholarly, in particular, the [1922]
Washington Conference, my knowledge of Ōmori and Yonai,[1] my property here and abroad, including bonds and financial status, my scholarly status, armed services, propa-
ganda activities, etc. Asked by a Board member, I gave a
brief report relative to my experiences since my evacuation,
condemning the condition of life and the treatment at Santa Anita, the more satisfactory conditions and treatment at
Tule Lake, and criticizing the procedures followed after my
arrest (the jail at Tule Lake and at Red Bluff). Everything
was far more satisfactory at Sharp Park. Mercado apolo-
gized about the jail and said that he was hoping for an early rectification of the jail aspect.

Then Treat was sworn to, and asked questions very similar, except that whether he shared views of the journalistic
war-mongers and whether he ever discussed with me the
possibility of war; the answers were in the negative. We were
held for one hour and 20 minutes while the German was held
ten minutes, Soki, 3 and Itagaki, 5. As soon as the formal
hearing was over, Mercado came out to the Waiting Room
and led me away to a corner and talked to me in a friendly
manner—[he said] the office failed to intern 6 Japanese who
should have been since he was positive that they were agents
of the Japanese Government. I asked his advice in regard to
getting extra clothes; he said, don't do it. Was this a hint of
the board's recommendation for my release? He said that I
would hear within three weeks which is necessary for bu-
reaucratic handling of the communication with the U.S. Attorney General [Francis] Biddle who decides.

Delays

In the 3rd week, Soki received the notice of his internment, and on the following morning, he was sent to the Fort Mc-Donald on Angel Island, the former San Francisco Immigration Station. On the 4th week, Itagaki got the notice of his release, and a week later he was sent to the Tule Lake Project, but notice came to me not until the 13th of October (41 days after the date of hearings); I was asked to fill the form used to communicate [with Tule Lake?] and determine the alleged truth of my former residence there, considered a necessary routine for which one week is consumed; I expected to depart on the 19th or 20th [of October] from the Sharp Park, but on the 16th (Saturday) at noon, I was told that the above form was lost and requested to fill [out] another. This was done, but the notice of departure did not come until 3:30 P.M. on the 26th (another 10 days were consumed).

Then I was told to pack up in haste since I had to leave the camp a little after 4 o'clock in order to catch the 6:30 train which was due at Klamath Falls at 6:30 A.M. of the 27th! [The three other Japanese] were sent on the 9:05 A.M. train; but the officers were anxious to dispatch me quickly after a long delay!

Note

1. Ōmori Takeo, a naval officer, attended Stanford before the war. According to the report on Ichihashi's hearing, the F.B.I. believed that Ōmori had been an active Japanese spy in the United States before returning to Japan; Report of the Hearing on Yamato Ichihashi, Sept. 3, 1942, Ichihashi SF INS File. Admiral Yonai Mitsumasa had been minister of the Imperial Navy and prime minister. Extremists in Japan actually considered Yonai, who had opposed the Tripartite Pact with the Axis powers, a moderate and had him replaced in July 1940. He later returned to the cabinet in 1944. He privately favored an early end to the war and was a member of what was known as the "peace faction."

The Break-Up of a Family

Amy Uno Ishii

Following are excerpts from an interview of former evacuee
Amy Uno Ishii conducted by Betty E. Mitson and Kristin
Mitchell for the California State University at Fullerton Japa-
nese American World War II Evacuation Oral History Project.
In the interview, Ishii recalls how she came home after learning of the attack on Pearl Harbor to find the FBI ransacking
her California home. When the agents were finished, they
took her father into custody and left. It was weeks before the
Ishii family learned that their father was being held in an old
Civilian Conservation Corps camp in Griffith Park in Los
Angeles. He was eventually sent to a camp for enemy aliens
in Missoula, Montana. Ishii also relates how difficult it was
for her family to adjust to life without her father, who was the
backbone of her family. For the duration of the war, Ishii's
father was transferred from camp to camp, finally earning his
release in 1947.

*K*ristin Mitchell: *Do you recall the day of the Pearl Harbor attack? Do you recall any special feelings you
had*?
  Amy Uno Ishii: Well, of course. I think we all went
through a terrible shock. On that Sunday morning I was living as a domestic away from home, and so I was not with
my own family. By that time I was almost twenty-one. I was
working as a domestic out in San Marino, and I had just
served breakfast to the family when the news came on the

radio that Japan had attacked Pearl Harbor. It's hard to describe the shock. I know that the American people were in great shock at the time of Pearl Harbor. And they were angry; they were very, very angry at the Japanese for having been so daring as this.

I remember that I asked my boss if I could make this long distance call to Los Angeles to talk to my mother because of the war having broken out. I asked him if I could have the day off and if I could go home to find out what this was all about. I made the call to my mother, and my mother was very, very upset. She said, "I don't understand what is happening, but I am hearing the news as you are hearing it on the radio there." She said, "I can't understand Japan and what it's doing bombing Pearl Harbor." We had no knowledge of anything like this happening, and it was just an absolute shock.

We had mixed emotions about the bombing. We were thinking, "Japan is committing suicide," because it is such a small country. All of Japan could be laid right across the whole of California, and it would be all over with. "What is that small country doing coming this long, long distance to do such crazy things?" And at the same time we were very upset because the general public. . . . Even the people that I worked for treated me and talked to me as though it was my own father who was piloting those planes out there at Pearl Harbor.

Oh, even the people you worked for treated you this way?

Yes. I remember they told me that I could go home and how I had better stay at home until the FBI could clear me of any suspicion. I said, "Why should I be suspected of anything? I've lived in your home for many years now, nursed you when you were sick and fed you. And I never poisoned you once, and I'm not about to do it now." But they said, "You had better stay at home until we can get the FBI to clear you." And I thought, "Wow!"

So I took the streetcar to my mother's. We got the news of Pearl Harbor's bombing just before noon, so it took me to three or four in the afternoon to get from the people's place in San Marino to my mother's.

Did you feel any animosity from some of the people you were riding on the streetcar with?

No. I think everyone was in too much of a state of shock to point their finger at me and say anything. I felt like an ant. I wanted to shrivel up into nothing, and my mind was going a mile a minute, thinking, "What am I supposed to do, what am I supposed to say? All I know is that I am an American, and yet now, at a time like this, people are going to say, 'You are a Jap,' and that turns the whole picture around." I had never been called a "Jap" in my life. All of these things were going through my mind. By the time I got home the FBI was at our house.

The FBI Investigation

What were they doing there?

They were tearing out the floorboards, taking bricks out of the fireplace, and looking through the attic.

What were they looking for?

Contraband.

Such as what?

Machine guns, munitions, maps, binoculars, cameras, swords, knives, and what have you.

How was your family reacting to this invasion?

Well, we just stood there—blah! What could we say with military police standing out in front with guns pointing at the house, and telling us to stay right there in a particular room while they went through the whole house? They tore part of the siding out on the side of our house to see if we were hiding things in between the walls. And all we could think was, "How ridiculous!" It was so nonsensical. They didn't have a search warrant. They didn't have any reason to be coming in like this and tearing up our house. And when they left, they took my father with them.

Did they conduct a general search of your neighborhood or was your house singled out?

We were singled out. There were no Japanese in our neighborhood. We were living in a cosmopolitan area; it was mostly white. Our next-door neighbors were Germans and Italians. The people across the street were from England. We had a Korean living on the corner of our block who had a little Korean grocery store. I would say that there weren't any Japanese living within six blocks of our house. So we must have been singled out.

So on the very day that Pearl Harbor was bombed your father was taken away?

Yes.

The Camp at Griffith Park

When did you hear from him next?

Oh, we didn't hear from him for a long, long time. We were getting all kinds of phone calls from people who were very good to us and who knew us very well. Say, for instance, on a Saturday night we got a phone call saying, "It would be a very good idea if you drove down to Griffith Park [in Los Angeles] tomorrow morning. Way inside of Griffith Park there is a Civilian Conservation Corps (CCC) camp, and this CCC camp is holding about three hundred men, and I think your father might be among them. So you might take a run down there and take a look." We really never knew who had called and told us.

On Sunday morning—instead of going to church—we all jumped in the car. We took toothpaste, soap, washcloths, underwear, pajamas, Hershey bars, chewing gum, and all kinds of things with us, and we took a ride out to Griffith Park. And sure enough, as we got way into Griffith Park, we found military police all around this encampment. All the men that had been picked up the first day of the war were rounded up in there; all were from this particular area. The people in the stockade, as we called it, were not allowed to converse among themselves because most of them didn't speak English.

Why didn't they converse in Japanese?

If they did, the MPs couldn't have understood them, so they were threatened to be shot to death if they spoke Japanese. We were very brave, and very young, so we stood out there on the sidelines of this enclosure and yelled, "Dad, Dad, if you recognize us, put your hands up." All of us were yelling in unison at these men. Of course, these men were dumbfounded. They didn't expect a family of young kids to come out and look for them. Of course, my father realized immediately that this couldn't be anyone but his bunch of kids, so he was waving his hand, saying, "Great." So then all of us took turns pitching.

What were you pitching to him?

Soap, toothpaste, his shaving kit and things. The MPs couldn't stop us.

Did they try to or did they just turn a blind eye to it?

Well, they didn't realize what was going on, because everything was happening so fast. We laughed about the whole thing later. But this was our first encounter with Dad since he was taken from us.

What was the time span involved?

About three weeks. I'm sure it was in January when we went to see him at Griffith Park.

Then another time we received a phone call saying, "It might be a good idea—if you know where the train station is in Glendale—for you to take a drive out there and just happen to be around." This was on a Sunday morning again. So on Sunday morning we packed a lot of stuff again, goodies, clothes, foodstuff, and things, and we got into the car and drove out to Glendale. We had a problem locating the train station. It was right off San Fernando Road—practically under our noses—but we drove around and asked at a few gas stations. We parked a block away and walked into the station there.

It all looked very normal—like any Sunday morning when there is very little happening. But about ten minutes after we arrived there, here came all these Army trucks with canopies over the backs of them. And in all these trucks were all these men out of the compound at Griffith Park. So we knew that our dad must be in this group. So we hid, not letting the military police see us. But then we realized what was happening—they were going to be shipped away on a train. They got off the trucks and were lined up, but they were not handcuffed or anything like that.

Did the soldiers have guns?

Oh, yes! When all of the men were lined up, our dad stood out like a sore thumb. He was very tall, and he had grown a beard. They were all looking so tired; all of those men looked so aged and tired, and when we saw our father, we just couldn't help but cry because the change in so short a time had been so drastic.

We didn't want Mother to see him like this because, I think, it probably would have just killed her on the spot. Fortunately, we hadn't brought Mother out with us. We figured that if we were going to get caught, at least we would be citizens being caught. Mother was an alien. If she got caught, we didn't know what they'd do with her, so we made her stay home. It was a long wait for her. We saw them line the men up and put tags on them with their I.D. numbers. They were all dressed in the same type of clothes—Army fatigues. We wondered where their regular clothes that they came in wearing were. A lot of those men were wearing suits when we saw them at Griffith Park.

How much time had elapsed since you saw them at Griffith Park?

Maybe a couple of weeks. I don't think the men's heads were shaven or anything like that. All I remember is that all of the men were wearing the same type of clothing. The first thing that flashes into your mind is the movies where you see prisoners wearing prisoners' garb, so that really shook us up. The men were lined up to go on these trains, so we yelled at Dad.

Didn't you get a chance to talk to him at all?

No, but he saw our faces, and he recognized each one of us. In fact, he hollered, "Hi, Hana. Hi, Mae. Hi, Amy. Be good, take care."

Fort Missoula, Montana

Did you have any idea where he was going?

Oh, no. In fact, no one knew where they were taken un-

til, I believe, we were in Santa Anita. After we were evacuated and were in Santa Anita, the Red Cross notified my
mother that Dad was in Fort Missoula in Montana.

Was he in a camp set up specifically for aliens?

It was a special camp for so-called hard core enemy aliens.

Was it just for Japanese?

Oh, yes, all Japanese. These camps held the men who
were fishermen out in Terminal Island and Long Beach and
all along the West Coast from Washington to Mexico. These
men were all pulled up out of their jobs because they
worked on the West Coast. They could send signals and
what have you. Oh, the American government thought these
people were going to commit sabotage. So they categorized
them as "hard core enemy aliens" and took these men away
from their families—took them just like they took my father.
There were approximately two thousand five hundred men
taken from their families in this manner—Japanese language
school teachers, judo teachers, kendo teachers, Buddhist
priests, anyone who worked in the import and export business with Japan—rounded up and taken away.

Due Process Denied

*So anyone who was considered dangerous in any sense was
taken?*

Yes. They were not given due process or anything—they
were just considered potentially dangerous.

People say that families were not being broken up. That's
a lot of malarkey; it happened to our own family. We know
how badly the families were broken up. We've seen too
many of our friends whose fathers were in the same situation as my father. A lot of the farmers up in Palos Verdes,
Rolling Hills, Signal Hill, Dominguez Hills, and Hunting-
ton Beach areas were taken away. If they were suspected of
anything at all, they were tagged "potentially dangerous enemy aliens," and taken. When you think of the number of
Japanese people that were rounded up in this fashion, you've
got to relate these numbers to the fact that each one of these
men had a family—a wife, and so many children. . . .

What feelings did you have as a family after they took your father away? Did you have any idea what was going to happen to your family?

Well, we really didn't know. We were in a state of shock for the longest time. We didn't know what was happening from one week to the next. The news would keep changing. There was a time when the news said, "If you people will be very good citizens and stay within a certain area of your residence, you will not be bothered." There was a very strict curfew law. We had to be in by five o'clock in the evening; we could not go out before a certain time in the morning; we could travel only so many miles away from our homes. If you worked a little further than that from your home, then you had to give up your job.

A Difficult Adjustment

How did the family feel about the absence of your father?

This was the most difficult thing, adjusting to having Dad away from home. My mother and father had just celebrated their twenty-fifth wedding anniversary, and after twenty-five years of being married and really not being separated in anyway, other than when my father was traveling as a salesman . . . but this was an understanding that they had with each other. Of course, mother was home with the children, but to have my father forcibly taken away from my mother. . . . It was the first time that they had ever been separated.

I imagine that she was in a state of shock.

She certainly was. Her blood pressure was really high, and it was a matter of trying to keep her composure. She realized that she now had to be the head of the household, the backbone of the family. It was very difficult when the little ones would say to my mother, "When is Daddy coming home? Where is he?" What kind of answers could she give?

Right, because she just didn't know.

Yes. Could she tell the children truthfully that Daddy will be gone only a couple of weeks or a couple of months or a couple of years? She didn't even know. And the children were very close to Dad, so they worried about him everyday. Of course, the mention of my father would just break my mother up, and it was just eating away at her. Then the evacuation order came. . . .

Evacuation

Did you have any idea where you were going to be?

Oh, no. No, that was really the biggest surprise of all. No one had any inkling as to where we were going to be sent and for how long. Of course, when the actual evacuation order was declared—President Roosevelt's Executive Order 9066—posters were put up along all of the telephone poles, fences, and any public place. No one could miss seeing these posters. Those original posters should be collectors' items today, if anyone saved them.

How much time did you have between announcement of Executive Order 9066 and the actual evacuation?

Well, we knew in February that we would eventually be evacuated. We didn't know just when, but there was a deadline. They offered us a chance to leave the West Coast voluntarily. Japanese people who had money, or businesses, and could liquidate all of their property and businesses could take their families and move voluntarily inland. Presumably, they would not be affected by the evacuation. Many of the Japanese people did this, only to find that when they got out of California and started to go in through Nevada and Arizona and the other states, the people in those states were waiting and saying, "You're not coming through our state.". . .

Where were you told to assemble?

We were told to assemble at the Centenary Methodist church on the corner of Thirty-fifth and Normandie. There was a group that assembled at the Hollywood Independent Church on Westmoreland and Lexington and one at the Union Church in Little Tokyo, in downtown Los Angeles. Depending on where you lived you were told to be at a particular place by 9 A.M. on a particular day. Then the trucks and the buses would roll up and take all your belongings. They tagged everything with your name. Then you got on these trucks and buses. From the minute we left our home to the time we arrived at Santa Anita Racetrack, we had no idea where we were going. . . .

The Family Is Separated

How long were you at Santa Anita?

Let's see, we were there the first week in April, 1942. I left Santa Anita the first of September to go to Heart Mountain, Wyoming. My mother, sisters and brothers were in Santa Anita until November of that year, when they were sent to Amache, Colorado.

Why were you sent to two different locations?

Well, it's like this. When we were in Santa Anita, I decided I was going to get married. So I got married in camp. . . .

Were you able to keep in touch with the rest of your family that was in the other camps?

Yes, we kept in touch. The family knew that I went to Heart Mountain because as soon as I arrived there I wrote to Santa Anita.

They hadn't known where you were going.

They didn't know where I was headed for, because the train that I was on went to all the other camps.

And they didn't tell you in advance?

No, we never knew in which camp we would eventually end up. When we got to wherever our destination was, it was our place to write to our family and let them know where we were. I didn't realize then that my mother, sisters and brothers had left Santa Anita to go to Amache, Colorado, until they got there and wrote me in Heart Mountain saying, "This is where we are."

Censored Correspondence

Did you hear from your father, too?

My father's contact with the family came by way of the Red Cross.

Oh, I see. But was he allowed to correspond personally?

No, not for a long time. It was at least six to eight months before we could get personal contact with my father. My mother was corresponding with him for awhile at the beginning, but all the letters were censored. I remember my mother sitting there with her first letter from my father. She opened up this beautiful letter that had already been ripped open and then Scotch-taped closed. She opened it very carefully, and set it down on a little table we had built. She opened this letter and pieces came out of it. She thought, "Wow, what's this? Is Daddy playing some kind of a joke on me?" We kind of put them together, and all we got was "and, but, so, how"—words, just words. Nothing of importance came out; nobody's name; no place—nothing. My mother sat there just completely exasperated. (laughter) That was her first contact with my father from Fort Missoula in Montana.

Did he stay in Fort Missoula the entire time?

No, he was sent from there to Lordsburg, New Mexico, and then to Santa Fe, New Mexico, and then to. . . . And in between—each time he changed camps—he was sent to a port of deportation. They sent him to Seattle once to get on some boat that was supposed to take him back to Japan, and he fought them. He said, "I refuse to go to Japan. You're not sending me to Japan. My life is here; my wife and my children are here. You're not sending me to Japan. You've got no reason to send me. Therefore, you've got to send me back to camp." So instead of sending him back to Fort Missoula they sent him to Lordsburg. From there they sent him to another place where he was supposed to catch a boat to Japan, and he fought them again. He said, "You're not sending me to Japan." So they sent him to Santa Fe. Then he went to Long Beach or someplace, and they were going to put him on a boat to send him to Japan. He said, "No way are you going to send me to Japan." By that time he had four sons in the service, and he said, "I've got boys fighting for this country; my wife is in camp, and my children are there. I have nothing to go to Japan for, and I refuse to go." So they sent him to Bismarck, North Dakota, and then they sent him from there to New Jersey to catch another boat.

He had extensive travels, didn't he?

Yes, and he was going to get on the *Gripsholm* ship in New Jersey, but he fought them again. He said, "There's no way that you're going to send me to Japan; I have nothing there. I would become a ward of the government if you sent me to Japan. How am I going to be able to provide for my wife and children, and I've got sons fighting in the service here." So instead of sending him back to Bismarck, North Dakota, they said, "Well, the only thing we can do in a case like this is to open up another camp."

And where was that?

This was in Crystal City, Texas. They made it into a family camp, where those men who were considered "hard core enemy aliens" could now join their wives. So my father went to Crystal City, and my mother and the minor children left Amache to join my father at Crystal City. This was the first time they had seen each other during all that time.

More American than Most

During this extensive process, did he ever receive any kind of a hearing or trial?

Well, apparently it was not what you would call a trial. It gave somebody or some people a job to do, and that was to go into these camps and interrogate the internees. I know that my father had been interrogated almost daily for months upon months. He had to lay down his whole life history from the time he was born to the present. What they were doing was actually trying to find out why they were holding him. They had to have a reason for keeping him.

So they were trying to find it after the fact.

Now that they had the person behind barbed wire, they asked, "Why do we have him here?" So they had to find a reason for keeping him there. That is what it all boils down to. At the very end they did admit to us though—to the family and to my father—that they really had no reason for keeping him. He was much more American than a lot of the Americans walking the main streets of any city today. He was more American politically, he knew the laws; he knew the Constitution, the by-laws, and the rights. He studied the United States government so extensively that he actually knew more about America than a lot of the men who were interrogating him. . . .

Did they ever give your father a hearing in front of a judge or a court hearing?

No, no court hearing.

No court hearing at all; they just interrogated him.

Yes.

Release

How long did they keep him after he was in Crystal City, Texas?

He came home to our family in September, 1947.

That was long after the rest of you had returned.

Yes, we had already been released from camp. I had been in Chicago from 1944 until 1946, then I came back to California to join my mother, sisters and brothers. My brothers, who had been overseas, were already back by that time. Lo and behold, in September, 1947 they finally decided to turn my father loose. He came home to us while we were living at the housing project known at that time as Roger Young Village, which was the quonset hut village out there behind Griffith Park. So he started out from Griffith Park and came back to Griffith Park.

Chapter 3

Evacuation

Chapter Preface

On February 19, 1942, President Franklin Roosevelt signed Executive Order 9066, authorizing General John L. DeWitt, head of the Western Defense Command, to remove Japanese residents from sensitive military areas. In March, DeWitt issued the first of a series of Civilian Exclusion Orders, requiring all persons of Japanese ancestry, regardless of citizenship, to evacuate the western portions of Washington, Oregon, and California, and the southern portion of Arizona, an area that DeWitt had designated Military Area Number One.

Japanese Americans were at first encouraged to relocate on their own. Three thousand Japanese residents, many of whom had relatives and friends in the midwest and on the East Coast, took advantage of the opportunity. The majority of Japanese, however, had lived their entire lives on the West Coast and had little prospect of being able to settle elsewhere. By the end of March, more than 100,000 Japanese remained on the Pacific shore and DeWitt was forced to conclude that voluntary relocation was a failure. Evacuation was declared compulsory and was to be conducted by the Army. Evacuation notices began to appear on telephone posts and in store windows instructing Japanese residents to pack only what they could carry and to report to designated departure points. In some cases, Japanese families were given as little as one week to make arrangements for the care or sale of a lifetime's collection of personal belongings. "You had to sell everything," recalls Yuri Tateishi, a resident of Torrance, California. "We were just limited to what we could take with us, and so everything was just sold for whatever we could get."

After Japanese residents disposed of the personal belongings they could not carry, they were transported under armed guard to temporary camps called assembly centers, where they were to reside until permanent camps could be finished. Many of these assembly centers were hastily converted racetracks where families were housed in horse stalls. Emi Somekawa, an evacuee from Portland, Oregon, writes: "There was so much horse and cow manure around. We were put into a cubicle that just had plywood walls and it was a horse stall with planks on the floor. . . . You'd find grass growing through the planks already, and it was just terrible." Though the assembly centers were only temporary shelters, the primitive conditions exacerbated the difficulties many Japanese faced during the relocation.

Evacuation Day

Monica Sone

> In the following essay, excerpted from her memoir *Nisei
> Daughter*, Monica Sone describes her family's experiences in
> preparing for evacuation from their Seattle home and their
> arrival at Camp Harmony, the assembly center in Puyallup,
> Washington. As her father made frantic preparations for the
> care of the family hotel, Sone, along with her mother, sister,
> and brother sorted through a lifetime accumulation of posses-
> sions to determine what was going to be packed and what was
> going to be left behind. After saying goodbye to the family
> home and dog, the Sones attempted to settle into the 18 x 20-
> foot room that served as their home for the next month.

General DeWitt kept reminding us that E day, evacuation
day, was drawing near. "E day will be announced in the
very near future. If you have not wound up your affairs by
now, it will soon be too late."

Father negotiated with Bentley Agent and Company to
hire someone to manage his business. Years ago Father had
signed a long-term lease with the owner of the building and
the agent had no other alternative than to let Father keep
control of his business until his time ran out. He was one of
the fortunate few who would keep their businesses intact for
the duration.

And Mother collected crates and cartons. She stayed up
night after night, sorting, and re-sorting a lifetime's accu-
mulation of garments, toys and household goods. Those
were pleasant evenings when we rummaged around in old

trunks and suitcases, reminiscing about the good old days, and almost forgetting why we were knee-deep in them.

Fast and Furious Orders

The general started issuing orders fast and furiously. "Everyone must be inoculated against typhoid and carry a card bearing the physician's signature as proof."

Like magic we all appeared at the old Japanese Chamber of Commerce building on Jackson Street and formed a long, silent queue inside the dark corridor, waiting to pass into the doctor's crowded office. The doctor's pretty young wife, pale and tired, helped her husband puncture the long line of bare brown arms.

On the twenty-first of April 1942, a Tuesday, the general gave us the shattering news. "All the Seattle Japanese will be moved to Puyallup by May 1. Everyone must be registered Saturday and Sunday between 8 A.M. and 5 P.M. They will leave next week in three groups, on Tuesday, Thursday and Friday."

Up to that moment, we had hoped against hope that something or someone would intervene for us. Now there was no time for moaning. A thousand and one details must be attended to in this one week of grace. Those seven days sputtered out like matches struck in the wind, as we rushed wildly about. Mother distributed sheets, pillowcases and blankets, which we stuffed into seabags. Into the two suitcases, we packed heavy winter overcoats, plenty of sweaters, woolen slacks and skirts, flannel pajamas and scarves. Personal toilet articles, one tin plate, tin cup and silverware completed our luggage. The one seabag and two suitcases apiece were going to be the backbone of our future home, and we planned it carefully.

Family 10710

Henry [the author's brother] went to the Control Station to register the family. He came home with twenty tags, all numbered "10710," tags to be attached to each piece of baggage, and one to hang from our coat lapels. From then on, we were known as Family # 10710.

On our last Sunday, Father and Henry moved all our furniture and household goods down to the hotel and stored them in one room. We could have put away our belongings in the government storage place or in the basement of our church, which was going to be boarded up for the duration, but we felt that our property would be safer under the watchful eyes of Sam, Peter and Joe [non-Japanese employees].

Monday evenings we received friends in our empty house where our voices echoed loudly and footsteps clattered woodenly on the bare floor. We sat on crates, drank bottles of coke and talked gayly about our future pioneer life. Henry and Minnie [Henry's girlfriend] held hands all evening in the corner of the living room. Minnie lived on the outskirts of the Japanese community and her district was to leave in the third and last group.

That night we rolled ourselves into army blankets like jelly rolls and slept on the bare floor. The next morning Henry rudely shouted us back into consciousness. "Six-thirty! Everybody wake up, today's the day!"

I screamed, "Must you sound so cheerful about it?"

"What do you expect me to do, bawl?"

On this sour note, we got up stiffly from the floor, and exercised violently to start circulation in our paralyzed backs and limbs. We jammed our blankets into the long narrow seabag, and we carefully tied the white pasteboard tag, 10710, on our coat lapels. When I went into the bathroom and looked into the mirror, tears suddenly welled in my eyes. I was crying, not because it was the last time I would be standing in a modern bathroom, but because I looked like a cross between a Japanese and a fuzzy bear. My hideous new permanent wave had been given to me by an operator who had never worked on Oriental hair before. My hair resembled scorched mattress filling, and after I had attacked it savagely with comb and brush, I looked like a frightened mushroom. On this morning of mornings when I was depending on a respectable hairdo so I could leave town with dignity, I was faced with this horror. There was nothing to do but cover it with a scarf.

Breakfast and Departure

Downstairs we stood around the kitchen stove where Mother served us a quick breakfast of coffee in our tin cups, sweet rolls and boiled eggs which rolled noisily on our tin plates. Henry was delighted with the simplicity of it all. "Boy, this is going to be living, no more company manners and dainty napkins. We can eat with our bare hands. Probably taste better, too."

Mother fixed a stern eye on Henry, "Not as long as I'm around."

The front doorbell rang. It was Dunks Oshima, who had offered to take us down to Eighth and Lane in a borrowed pickup truck. Hurriedly the menfolk loaded the truck with the last few boxes of household goods which Dunks was going to take down to the hotel. He held up a gallon can of soy sauce, puzzled, "Where does this go, to the hotel, too?"

Nobody seemed to know where it had come from or where it was going, until Mother finally spoke up guiltily, "Er, it's going with me. I didn't think we'd have shoyu where we're going."

Henry looked as if he were going to explode. "But Mama, you're not supposed to have more than one seabag and two suitcases. And of all things, you want to take with you— shoyu!"

I felt mortified. "Mama, people will laugh at us. We're not going on a picnic!"

But Mother stood her ground. "Nonsense. No one will ever notice this little thing. It isn't as if I were bringing liquor!"

"Well!" I said. "If Mama's going to take her shoyu, I'm taking my radio along." I rescued my fifteen-year-old radio from the boxes which were going down to the hotel. "At least it'll keep me from talking to myself out there."

Sumi [the author's sister] began to look thoughtful, and she rummaged among the boxes. Henry bellowed, "That's enough! Two suitcases and one seabag a person, that's final! Now let's get going before we decide to take the house along with us."

"Good-By House"

Mother personally saw to it that the can of shoyu remained with her baggage. She turned back once more to look at our brown and yellow frame house and said almost gayly, "Good-by, house."

Old Asthma came bounding out to the front yard, her tail swaying in the air. "And good-by, Asthma, take good care of our home. *Yoroshiku onegai shimasu yo.*". . .

"Quarter to eight," Dunks gently reminded us. We took turns ruffling Asthma's fur and saying good-by to her. The new tenants had promised us that they would keep her as their pet.

We climbed into the truck, chattering about the plucky little swallow. As we coasted down Beacon Hill bridge for the last time, we fell silent, and stared out at the delicately flushed morning sky of Puget Sound. We drove through bustling Chinatown, and in a few minutes arrived on the corner of Eighth and Lane. This area was ordinarily lonely and deserted but now it was gradually filling up with silent, labeled Japanese, standing self-consciously among their seabags and suitcases.

Everyone was dressed casually, each according to his idea of where he would be going. One Issei was wearing a thick mackinaw jacket and cleated, high-topped hiking boots. I stared admiringly at one handsome couple, standing slim and poised in their ski clothes. They looked newly wed. They stood holding hands beside their streamlined luggage that matched smartly with the new Mr. and Mrs. look. With an air of resigned sacrifice, some Issei [first generation Japanese American] women wore dark-colored slacks with deep-hemmed cuffs. One gnarled old grandmother wore an ankle-length black crepe dress with a plastic initial "S" pinned to its high neckline. It was old-fashioned, but dignified and womanly.

The Soldiers

Automobiles rolled up to the curb, one after another, discharging more Japanese and more baggage. Finally at ten o'clock, a vanguard of Greyhound busses purred in and parked themselves neatly along the curb. The crowd stirred and murmured. The bus doors opened and from each, a soldier with rifle in hand stepped out and stood stiffly at attention by the door. The murmuring died. It was the first time I had seen a rifle at such close range and I felt uncomfortable. This rifle was presumably to quell riots, but contrarily, I felt riotous emotion mounting in my breast.

Jim Shigeno, one of the leaders of the Japanese-American Citizens' League, stepped briskly up front and started reading off family numbers to fill the first bus. Our number came up and we pushed our way out of the crowd. Jim said, "Step right in." We bumped into each other in nervous haste. I glanced nervously at the soldier and his rifle, and I was startled to see that he was but a young man, pink-cheeked, his clear gray eyes staring impassively ahead. I felt that the occasion probably held for him a sort of tense anxiety as it did for us. Henry found a seat by a window and hung out,

Japanese evacuated to detainment camps were tagged with family numbers.

watching for Minnie who had promised to see him off. Sumi and I suddenly turned maternal and hovered over Mother and Father to see that they were comfortably settled. They were silent.

Newspaper photographers with flash-bulb cameras pushed busily through the crowd. One of them rushed up to our bus, and asked a young couple and their little boy to step out and stand by the door for a shot. They were reluctant, but the photographers were persistent and at length they got out of the bus and posed, grinning widely to cover their embarrassment. We saw the picture in the newspaper shortly after and the caption underneath it read, "Japs good-natured about evacuation."

Our bus quickly filled to capacity. All eyes were fixed up front, waiting. The guard stepped inside, sat by the door, and nodded curtly to the gray-uniformed bus driver. The door closed with a low hiss. We were now the Wartime Civil Control Administration's babies. . . .

Puyallup

We sped out of the city southward along beautiful stretches of farmland, with dark, newly turned soil. In the beginning we devoured every bit of scenery which flashed past our window and admired the massive-muscled work horses plodding along the edge of the highway, the rich burnished copper color of a browsing herd of cattle, the vivid spring green of the pastures, but eventually the sameness of the country landscape palled on us. We tried to sleep to escape from the restless anxiety which kept bobbing up to the surface of our minds. I awoke with a start when the bus filled with excited buzzing. A small group of straw-hatted Japanese farmers stood by the highway, waving at us. I felt a sudden warmth toward them, then a twinge of pity. They would be joining us soon.

About noon we crept into a small town. Someone said, "Looks like Puyallup [site of an assembly center in Washington], all right." Parents of small children babbled excitedly, "Stand up quickly and look over there. See all the chick-chicks and fat little piggies?" One little city boy stared hard at the hogs and said tersely, "They're *bachi*—dirty!"

Our bus idled a moment at the traffic signal and we noticed at the left of us an entire block filled with neat rows of low shacks, resembling chicken houses. Someone commented on it with awe, "Just look at those chicken houses. They sure go in for poultry in a big way here." Slowly the bus made a left turn, drove through a wire-fenced gate, and to our dismay, we were inside the oversized chicken farm. The bus driver opened the door, the guard stepped out and stationed himself at the door again. Jim, the young man who had shepherded us into the busses, popped his head inside and sang out, "Okay, folks, all off at Yokohama, Puyallup."

Camp Harmony

We stumbled out, stunned, dragging our bundles after us. It must have rained hard the night before in Puyallup, for we sank ankle deep into gray, gluttinous mud. The receptionist, a white man, instructed us courteously, "Now, folks, please stay together as family units and line up. You'll be assigned your apartment."

We were standing in Area A, the mammoth parking lot of the state fairgrounds. There were three other separate areas, B, C and D, all built on the fair grounds proper, near the baseball field and the race tracks. This camp of army barracks was hopefully called Camp Harmony.

We were assigned to apartment 2–1-A, right across from the bachelor quarters. The apartments resembled elongated, low stables about two blocks long. Our home was one room, about 18 by 20 feet, the size of a living room. There was one small window in the wall opposite the one door. It was bare except for a small, tinny wood-burning stove crouching in the center. The flooring consisted of two by fours laid directly on the earth, and dandelions were already pushing their way up through the cracks. Mother was delighted when she saw their shaggy yellow heads. "Don't anyone pick them. I'm going to cultivate them."

Father snorted, "Cultivate them! If we don't watch out, those things will be growing out of our hair.". . .

Settling In

Sumi reclined on her seabag and fretted, "Where do we sleep? Not on the floor, I hope."

"Stop worrying," Henry replied disgustedly.

Mother and Father wandered out to see what the other folks were doing and they found people wandering in the mud, wondering what other folks were doing. Mother returned shortly, her face lit up in an ecstatic smile, "We're in luck. The latrine is right nearby. We won't have to walk blocks.". . .

We cheered loudly when trucks rolled by, distributing canvas army cots for the young and hardy, and steel cots for the older folks. Henry directed the arrangement of the cots. Father and Mother were to occupy the corner nearest the wood stove. In the other corner, Henry arranged two cots in L shape and announced that this was the combination living room-bedroom area, to be occupied by Sumi and myself. He fixed a male den for himself in the corner nearest the door. If I had had my way, I would have arranged everyone's cots in one neat row as in Father's hotel dormitory.

We felt fortunate to be assigned to a room at the end of the barracks because we had just one neighbor to worry about. The partition wall separating the rooms was only seven feet high with an opening of four feet at the top, so at night, Mrs. Funai next door could tell when Sumi was still sitting up in bed in the dark, putting her hair up. "*Mah*, Sumi-*chan*," Mrs. Funai would say through the plank wall, "are you curling your hair tonight again? Do you put it up every night?" Sumi would put her hands on her hips and glare defiantly at the wall. . . .

My Citizenship Wasn't Real

All through the night I heard people getting up, dragging cots around. I stared at our little window, unable to sleep. I was glad Mother had put up a makeshift curtain on the window for I noticed a powerful beam of light sweeping across it every few seconds. The lights came from high towers placed around the camp where guards with Tommy guns kept a twenty-four hour vigil. I remembered the wire fence encircling us, and a knot of anger tightened in my breast. What was I doing behind a fence like a criminal? If there were accusations to be made, why hadn't I been given a fair trial? Maybe I wasn't considered an American anymore. My citizenship wasn't real, after all. Then what was I? I was certainly not a citizen of Japan as my parents were. On second thought, even Father and Mother were more alien residents of the United States than Japanese nationals for they had little tie with their mother country. In their twenty-five years in America, they had worked and paid their taxes to their adopted government as any other citizen.

Of one thing I was sure. The wire fence was real. I no longer had the right to walk out of it. It was because I had Japanese ancestors. It was also because some people had little faith in the ideas and ideals of democracy. They said that after all these were but words and could not possibly insure loyalty. New laws and camps were surer devices. I finally buried my face in my pillow to wipe out burning thoughts and snatch what sleep I could.

The Day We Were Kicked Out of Berkeley

Charles Kikuchi

> Following are excerpts from the journal of Berkeley student
> Charles Kikuchi, in which he describes the scene at the
> departure point for Japanese evacuees from the San Francisco
> area and his family's arrival at the Tanforan assembly center
> outside of San Bruno, California. Kikuchi depicts the surpris-
> ing lack of sadness among the American-born Japanese
> (Nisei), who seemed to be preparing for evacuation as if it
> were a vacation. Upon their arrival at Tanforan, a racetrack
> until it was hastily converted to an assembly center, Kikuchi
> and his family set about trying to make a livable home in the
> crowded and chaotic atmosphere.

A pril 30, 1942, Berkeley: Today is the day that we are going to get kicked out of Berkeley. It certainly is degrad-
ing. I am down here in the control station [collecting points for
Japanese Americans awaiting evacuation to assembly centers]
and I have nothing to do so I am jotting down these notes! The
Army Lieutenant over there doesn't want any of the photographers to take pictures of these miserable people waiting for
the Greyhound bus because he thinks that the American public might get a sympathetic attitude towards them.

I'm supposed to see my family at Tanforan as Jack [the
author's brother] told me to give the same family number. I

wonder how it is going to be living with them as I haven't done this for years and years? I should have gone over to San Francisco and evacuated with them, but I had a last final to take. I understand that we are going to live in the horse stalls. I hope that the Army has the courtesy to remove the manure first.

"Have a Nice Time"

This morning I went over to the bank to close my account and the bank teller whom I have never seen before solemnly shook my hand and he said, "Goodbye, have a nice time." I wonder if that isn't the attitude of the American people? They don't seem to be bitter against us, and I certainly don't think I am any different from them. That General De Witt certainly gripes my ass because he has been listening to the Associated Farmers[1] too much.

Oh, oh, there goes a "thing" in slacks and she is taking pictures of that old Issei [first generation Japanese American] lady with a baby. She says she is the official photographer, but I think she ought to leave these people alone. The Nisei around here don't seem to be so sad. They look like they are going on a vacation. They are all gathered around the bulletin board to find out the exact date of their departure. "When are you leaving?" they are saying to one another. Some of those old Issei men must have gone on a binge last night because they smell like *sake* [rice wine].

Mitch [Kunitani, a friend of Kikuchi's] just came over to tell us that I was going on the last bus out of Berkeley with him. Oh, how lucky I am! The Red Cross lady just told me that she would send a truck after my baggage and she wants the phone number. I never had a phone in that dump on Haste Street.

I have a queer sensation and it doesn't seem real. There are smiling faces all around me and there are long faces and gloomy faces too. All kinds of Japanese and Caucasian faces

1. The Associated Farmers was a trade association of generally well-off California farmers; it had actively urged the relocation of the Japanese (who were in many instances competitors of theirs).

around this place. Soon they will be neurotic cases. Wang [Warren Tsuneishi, a friend of Kikuchi's] thinks that he has an empty feeling in his stomach and I told him to go get a hamburger upstairs because the Church people are handing out free food. I guess this is a major catastrophe so I guess we deserve some free concessions.

The Church people around here seem so nice and full of consideration saying, "Can we store your things?" "Do you need clothes?" "Sank you," the Issei smile even now though they are leaving with hearts full of sorrow. But the Nisei around here seem pretty bold and their manners are brazen. They are demanding service. I guess they are taking advantage of their college educations after all. "The Japs are leaving, hurrah, hurrah!" some little kids are yelling down the

Ghost Town

Following is an excerpt from a letter written by Berkeley student Charles Kikuchi to a friend in which he describes the conditions in San Francisco's Japanese neighborhood in the days leading up to evacuation.

S.F. [San Francisco] Japanese Town certainly looks like a ghost town. All the stores are closed and the windows are bare except for a mass of "evacuation sale" signs. The junk dealers are having a roman holiday, since they can have their cake and eat it too. It works like this! They buy cheap from the Japanese leaving and sell dearly to the Okies coming in for defense work. Result, good profit. Lots of kids getting married off on the theory that they have to protect their vested interest when and if morals get loose in camp, but I don't think there is much danger of that happening, although the rowdier bunches will probably get rowdier for a while if they have nothing to do.

The Kikuchi Diary: Chronicle from an American Concentration Camp: The Tanforan Journals of Charles Kikuchi, John Modell, ed. Urbana: University of Illinois Press, 1973.

street but everybody ignores them. Well, I have to go up to the campus and get the results of my last exam and will barely be able to make it back here in time for the last bus. God, what a prospect to look forward to living among all those Japs!

May 3, 1942, Sunday: The whole family pitched in to build our new home at Tanforan. We raided the clubhouse[2] and tore off the linoleum from the bar table and put it on our floor so that it now looks rather homelike. Takeshi [Tom, the author's brother] works pretty hard for a little guy and makes himself useful, but the gals are not so useful. They'd rather wander around looking for the boys. However, they pitched in and helped clean up the new messhall so that we could have our meals there instead of walking all the way over to the clubhouse. It's about 11:00 now and everyone has gone to bed. You can hear the voices all the way down the barracks—everything sounds so clear. Tom just stepped out to water his "victory garden." The community spirit is picking up rapidly and everyone seems willing to pitch in. They had a meeting tonight to get volunteers for cooks and waiters at the new messhall and this was done without difficulty. Rules were also made for each barracks such as radio off at 10:00 and not too many lights so that the fuse would not get overloaded.

It Reminds Me of a Concentration Camp

We have only been here three days, but it already seems like weeks. Everyone here has fallen into the regular routine, without any difficult adjustments except Pop who was a problem child this morning. He got mad because he was not getting the proper food[3] so he went off by himself and got lost.

There are still many problems to be solved such as heating, cleaner dishes, more variety of foods, recreational, and other social problems but they will most likely be settled in time.

I saw a soldier in a tall guardhouse near the barbed wire

---

2. Tanforan had until quite recently been operated as a racetrack, and had been "converted" to residential use only hastily.   3. The elder Kikuchi required a special diet because of his diabetic condition.

fence and did not like it because it reminds me of a concentration camp. I am just wondering what the effects will be on the Japanese so cut off from the world like this. Within the confines of Tanforan our radios and papers are the only touch with reality. I hardly know how the war is going now, and it is so significant that the Allied forces win even though that will not mean that democracy will by any means be perfect or even justified. The whole post war period is going to be something terrific. Sometimes I feel like a foreigner in this camp hearing so much Japanese although our family uses English almost exclusively.

Taro [Katayama, editor of the camp newspaper] lives up in the Men's dormitory, the majority of whom are Issei, and he has a big American flag over his head for identification. I wonder what the Issei think of this. I haven't heard any talk about a "Japanese victory" although it must go on. You just can't change a group overnight, especially in the face of the fact that the Japanese have been so discriminated against in this state—witness the long history of anti-orientalism.

Drawing Together

We are planning to get the paper underway as soon as possible. It is needed now as a "morale raiser" and also for the information service that it could render. With 4000 more people coming in next week, the confusion may grow greater.

From an individual standpoint our family has not lost anything. We have been drawn close together as a group and everyone seems cheerful enough. Jack is straining a bit because of Helen [Jack's wife], I suppose, but he doesn't say too much. I tried to get him interested in the Medical Department here, but he was not too enthusiastic. He did show an interest in the library though. Tom and Miyako [the author's sister] are having a grand vacation. I hope they do not delay in setting up an efficient school system—education is so important for the future.

An Unwilling Journey

Daisuke Kitagawa

When General John L. DeWitt issued the evacuation order for
Japanese residents of the West Coast, many Japanese families
had just a few weeks to make arrangements for the care or
sale of their personal belongings. Since they were only
allowed to take what they could carry, numerous Japanese
Americans had to sell a lifetime's collection of personal
belongings at far below value. In the following essay, Daisuke
Kitagawa, a minister at St. Paul's Church in Kent, Washington, describes the many private auctions in which poverty-
stricken Japanese farmers sold their possessions to their creditors and other greedy buyers for practically nothing. After
liquidating their possessions, Kitagawa's community boarded
a train, under armed guard, for the Pinedale assembly center
near Fresno, California.

On Mother's Day weekend (May 10–12), 1942, we who
were living in the White River Valley [in Washington]
and its surrounding areas found ourselves on the evacuation
trains, destination unknown. I had been busy until the very
last minute handling countless details—legal, financial, domestic, personal—for my helpless companions. For example, it had taken endless negotiations with a number of agencies to secure permission for one tubercular patient to stay
in the sanatorium. On the day before the first train was to
leave, I had happened to meet at the hospital a young Nisei
[second generation Japanese American] woman, married to
a Filipino, who had just had a baby. Neither she nor her hus-

Excerpted from *Issei and Nisei: The Internment Years*, by Daisuke Kitagawa (New York:
The Seabury Press, 1967). Reprinted by permission of the Domestic and Foreign Mis-
sionary Society of the Protestant Episcopal Church USA.

band knew for sure whether she and their children were entitled to stay where they were or, if they had to be evacuated, whether her husband was entitled to accompany them to camp. The evacuation order was quite clear on that point: anyone of Japanese blood, of whatever degree, must be evacuated. Whether this resulted in a temporary separation of that man from his wife and children or whether he accompanied his family to the camp, I no longer remember. Most likely the young mother and her children caught one of the three trains while her husband remained behind, hoping that in the not-too-distant future arrangements could be made for their reunion.

Preliminaries of Departure

Prior to departure every family and every individual had to be registered. When registration was completed, each family or individual was given a family number.

The official instructions advised each person to take with him only as much as he could carry. The rest of his belongings were to be sold or left behind. The Wartime Civilian Control Administration (WCCA) provided a warehouse where anything we wanted to keep could be stored for the duration, free of charge. Most of our families were rather poor farmers, few owned furniture really worth storing, and most of them had debts which they managed to pay off by selling the greater part of their belongings. We had also converted our mission building into a storehouse where families might bring their things. As for myself, I did not own anything except books that needed special care. I put my library together and sent it to my good friend Lewis Bailey, the rector of Trinity Parish, Seattle. What few clothes and things of that sort I owned, were neatly put in a small trunk, which I left with Deaconess Peppers. My own problem was thus extremely simple. But a family who had lived in one place for ten, twenty, or thirty years, with five or six or, in some cases, even seven or eight children, heavily in debt and without resources, had only one choice: to sell everything they could not take with them.

Consequently, there were hundreds of private auctions go-

Evacuated Japanese families were only allowed to take what they could carry. All other possessions had to be sold or left behind.

ing on simultaneously all over the Valley, at which poverty-stricken Japanese farmers were parting with most of their worldly possessions as their creditors and other greed-ridden buyers purchased them for practically nothing. Those not in debt hastily liquidated large items like pianos, refrigerators, davenports, automobiles, and tractors. Some were fortunate enough, to be sure, to have long-standing and trustworthy neighbors or friends among Caucasian Americans—how regrettable that that phrase need be used—who would look after such things for them; and in some instances, these friends became caretakers of homes and farms—lock, stock, and barrel. Such cases, however, were not numerous. In addition, many could not bring themselves to trust the government and generally did not take advantage of the provisions for free storage because they feared that after they had been evacuated, somebody would set fire to the buildings in which their precious possessions were stored. How could anybody assure them that no such thing would happen, after what had already occurred despite all the assurances and reassurances given by people in whom they had placed their full confidence? "Convert everything saleable into cash while it can be done!" became the motto of many.

No Future

What this action meant in legal and economic terms, no one had even begun to comprehend. Few gave a thought to the fact that sooner or later the war would be over and a normal state of affairs would be restored. Everybody was preoccupied with the urgent problems that lay immediately ahead of them: what to do with what had been accumulated over the years, with all those precious things they were not to be allowed to take with them. Everybody worried about what their lives would be in the concentration camps. The aged men, especially, jumped to the conclusion that their sweat and toil of many years was now coming to naught and that

Prowling Like Wolves

When the evacuation order was issued, many Japanese families had as little as one week to dispose of their personal possessions. Unscrupulous furniture dealers often took advantage of this situation by offering Japanese residents prices for their goods that were far below value. In the following excerpt from Farewell to Manzanar, *Jeanne Wakatsuki Houston's memoir of the Japanese relocation, the author describes her mother's reaction to a dealer's low bid for a set of fine china.*

The secondhand dealers had been prowling around for weeks, like wolves, offering humiliating prices for goods and furniture they knew many of us would have to sell sooner or later. Mama had left all but her most valuable possessions in Ocean Park, simply because she had nowhere to put them. She had brought along her pottery, her silver, heirlooms like the kimonos Granny had brought from Japan, tea sets, lacquered tables, and one fine old set of china, blue and white porcelain, almost translucent. On the day we were leaving, Woody's [the author's brother] car was so crammed they were finished, absolutely finished. There would be no future for them in America. Whatever might happen in the years to follow, they were sure they would not have a chance to reclaim what they were then about to lose.

Being thoroughly Oriental, the Japanese made no noise and showed no visible signs of distress, even though many were frantic. They lost all their business sense and reasoning capacity, and, of course, they were amply taken advantage of. Some were relieved when they had sold off the last item in their houses. Not a few, for the first time in years, had cash in their pockets instead of a batch of loan notes.

Blind Journey

On May 12, which was Mother's Day, Fred Meadowcroft drove me to Renton in the old station wagon in which I used

---

with boxes and luggage and kids we had just run out of room. Mama had to sell this china.

One of the dealers offered her fifteen dollars for it. She said it was a full setting for twelve and worth at least two hundred. He said fifteen was his top price.

Mama started to quiver. Her eyes blazed up at him. . . . She didn't say another word. She just glared at this man, all the rage and frustration channeled at him through her eyes.

He watched her for a moment and said he was sure he couldn't pay more than seventeen fifty for that china. She reached into the red velvet case, took out a dinner plate and hurled it at the floor right in front of his feet.

The man leaped back shouting, "Hey! Hey, don't do that! Those are valuable dishes!"

Mama took out another dinner plate and hurled it at the floor, then another and another, never moving, never opening her mouth, just quivering and glaring at the retreating dealer, with tears streaming down her cheeks. He finally turned and scuttled out the door, heading for the next house.

Jeanne Wakatsuki Houston and James D. Houston, *Farewell to Manzanar.* New York: Bantam, 1973.

to collect and deliver children before and after Sunday school. Then I turned the car over to him, so that he might dispose of it for the diocese. I had two fair-sized suitcases and a bedroll.

At the Renton railway station, quite a crowd of people gathered to bid us farewell. That to me was a reassuring scene, and made an indelible impression on me. These people had been neighbors and business associates of our families, or schoolmates of our children. They were there as friends whose friendship could not be destroyed. Surrounding us were the fields and hills of the White River Valley, so fresh in their green under the warm sun of mid-May. Presently the train started to move silently. Once more good-byes were exchanged, and the distance between those standing by the tracks and those on the train increased by the second. For quite a number of people on that train, this was the last time they would ever see the Valley.

When it came time for us to depart, we were divided into three groups, the first of which left on May 10. Without hesitation I decided to go with the last group, because I wanted to be available in case of emergency or mishap. I had no fear about the camp to which we were going, having seen what an assembly center was like at Puyallup, though we did not have the faintest idea where it might be.

Pinedale

A number of soldiers, who functioned more or less as conductors, accompanied us. They were all young fellows, most of them friendly and easy to talk to. Soon we were told that all window shades had to be pulled and kept down all the time, without any reason being given. I walked from one end of the long train to the other, just to see how everybody was getting along. When I finally sat down and relaxed for the first time in many days, I immediately fell asleep. But soon I was awakened by children singing; and, lo and behold, the people around me were busy enjoying their lunch. Everybody was settled in his seat, relaxed and looking as if he hadn't a thing in the world to worry about.

No one seemed to care where we were being taken. No matter what might be ahead of us, we were all together; and that was the most reassuring thing for the moment. Thus, quite unexpectedly, we had a rather enjoyable journey for, I believe, two days and two nights. It brought us to Pinedale, a few miles outside Fresno, California, which turned out to be our destination.

What time of the day it was when we arrived, I do not remember. From the railroad station we were driven in Army trucks to a place with rows and rows of barracks inside barbed-wire fences. There was inspection of baggage once again, presumably to make sure that no one carried into the camp any contraband articles: short-wave radio sets, firearms, or firewater. Then each family was given one room, into which as many Army cots were brought as there were numbers in the family. There was no other furniture whatever. Single men were steered into bachelors' barracks, a fate which I escaped because I was a clergyman. No one raised any fuss about my receiving such special treatment, and it was not long before I began to have a constant stream of people visiting me with all sorts of complaints and entreating me to present their cases to the camp administration.

The Pain of Relocation

Mary Tsukamoto

In the following essay, Mary Tsukamoto, a resident of Florin, California, at the time of the Japanese attack on Pearl Harbor, recalls her experience during the evacuation of Japanese residents from the West Coast. As a member of the Japanese American Citizens League (JACL), Tsukamoto tried her best to help Japanese residents comply with relocation orders, despite the confusing and often conflicting instructions issued by government officials. In addition to coping with her own fears, Tsukamoto offered spiritual comfort to other members of the Japanese community suffering from the stress of having to leave their lives behind. Tsukamoto describes the grief endured by the Japanese community when it was learned that neighborhoods and communities were going to be split up in the coming relocation.

I do remember Pearl Harbor day. I was about twenty-seven, and we were in church. It was a December Sunday, so we were getting ready for our Christmas program. We were rehearsing and having Sunday School class, and I always played the piano for the adult Issei [first generation Japanese American] service. Of course, because there were so many Japanese, all of it was in Japanese; the minister was a Japanese, and he preached in Japanese. But after the service started, my husband ran in. He had been home that day and heard on the radio. We just couldn't believe it, but he told us that Japan attacked Pearl Harbor. I remember how stunned we were. And suddenly the whole world turned

Excerpted from "Jerome," by Mary Tsukamoto, in *And Justice for All: An Oral History of the Japanese American Detention Camps*, by John Tateishi. Copyright ©1984 by John Tateishi. Reprinted by permission of the University of Washington Press.

dark. We started to speak in whispers, and because of our experience [with anti-Japanese sentiment] in Florin, we immediately sensed something terrible was going to happen. We just prayed that it wouldn't, but we sensed the things would be very difficult. The minister and all of the leaders discussed matters, and we knew that we needed to be prepared for the worst.

Then, of course, within a day or two, we heard that the FBI had taken Mr. Tanigawa and Mr. Tsuji. I suppose the FBI had them on their list, and it wasn't long before many of them were taken. We had no idea what they were going through. We should have been more aware. One Issei, Mr. Iwasa, committed suicide. So all of these reports and the anguish and the sorrow made the whole world very dark. Then rumors had it that we were supposed to turn in our cameras and our guns, and they were called in. Every day there was something else about other people being taken by the FBI. Then gradually we just couldn't believe the newspapers and what people were saying. And then there was talk about sending us away, and we just couldn't believe that they would do such a thing. It would be a situation where the whole community would be uprooted. But soon enough we were reading reports of other communities being evacuated from San Pedro and from Puget Sound. After a while we became aware that maybe things weren't going to just stop but would continue to get worse and worse.

A Fearful Experience

We read about President Roosevelt's Executive Order 9066. I remember the Japanese American Citizens League (JACL) people had a convention in San Francisco in March. We realized that we needed to be able to rise to the occasion to help in whatever way we could in our community. We came home trying to figure out just how we could do that. We had many meetings at night and the FBI was always lurking around. We were told we couldn't stay out after eight o'clock in the evening.

Meanwhile, Hakujin [white] neighbors were watching us

The USS Nevada *was the only battleship to get underway during the Japanese attack on Pearl Harbor.*

and reporting to the FBI that we were having secret meetings. We were not supposed to meet after eight o'clock, but often we couldn't cut off our JACL meeting at eight o'clock, and so we would have tea or coffee and keep talking. We would be reported, and the police would come. There were so many people making life miserable for us. Then we heard that we had been restricted to traveling five miles from our homes; it was nine miles to Sacramento, and at that time everything was in Sacramento, like doctors, banks, and grocery stores. So it just was a terrible, fearful experience. Every time we went anywhere more than five miles away, we were supposed to go to the Wartime Civilian Control Administration (WCCA) office in Sacramento, nine miles away, to get a permit. It was ridiculous.

A lot of little things just nagged at us and harassed us, and we were frightened, but even in that atmosphere I remember we frantically wanted to do what was American. We were Americans and loyal citizens, and we wanted to do what Americans should be doing. So we were wrapping Red Cross bandages and trying to do what we could to help our country. By May 1942, more than a hundred of our boys were already drafted. We worried about them, and they were worried about what was going to happen to their families. We knew what we wanted to do. We started to buy war bonds, and we took first aid classes with the rest of the Hakujin people in the community. We went out at night to go to these classes, but we worried about being out after eight o'clock. It was a frightening time. Every little rule and regulation was imposed only on the Japanese people. There were Italian and German people in the community, but it was just us that had travel restrictions and a curfew. . . .

And we were still trying to think about how we could serve the community. I finally opened a JACL office near the end of March, and I was running in and out of the WCCA office. They finally decided to send some people out to work with me to advise me and the welfare office and the Federal Reserve Bank and the Farm Security Agency. They were to help the people who were asking questions and trying to get ready for this terrible ordeal that was ahead of them. Not knowing for sure, many of them kept hoping and wishing that we would not have to go, that somehow things would change and we wouldn't have to leave.

Confusion

We tried to get everybody instructions, and the WCCA would tell me one thing one day, and I would then tell everybody this is what we're going to need to do, and then the next week the whole regulation was changed, and we just ended up being liars right and left. It was such a state of confusion and anger, everyone being so upset at what was happening. I remember I was crying inside and I just felt like I was put through a hamburger machine. I was human and worried and scared for myself too, but worried about everybody else and trying to help people.

I remember Ida Onga. Her husband was taken by the FBI, and she came in here so big; she was going to have a baby in a month or so. She cried because she was supposed to go and see the doctor, and she didn't know that she had to have a traveler's permit. She had come from Folsom and had traveled more than five miles. I needed to get her into town so she could get to the doctor, and so I took her to the WCCA office for a travel permit. There we found out that Mrs. Tsuji's husband was taken away by the FBI. But nobody thought about the family left behind needing food and money. We finally arranged for the WCCA welfare office to provide food, and she cried because Japanese people are proud and they weren't willing to accept handouts. They never had been on welfare before, and she felt terrible because here she ended up receiving food. But we told her this was different, because her husband was taken and because it's what you have to do. She had three children. These things were happening.

I remember Mrs. Kuima, whose son was thirty-two years old and retarded. She took care of him. They had five other boys, but she took care of this boy at home. The welfare office said No, she couldn't take him, that the families have to institutionalize a child like that. It was a very tragic thing for me to have to tell her, and I remember going out to the field—she was hoeing strawberries—and I told her what they told us, that you can't take your son with you. And so she cried, and I cried with her. A few days before they were evacuated they came to take him away to an institution. It was very hard for me to face that family. I felt as though I was the messenger that carried such tragic news for them. It was only about a month after we got to Fresno Assembly Center that they sent us a wire saying he died. All these years she loved him and took care of him, he only knew Japanese and ate Japanese food. I was thinking of the family; they got over it quietly; they endured it. I just felt guilty, you know, just for having been involved.

The Anxiety of Evacuation

I had anxieties for Grandpa and Grandma. They were old and had farmed all their lives, and after more than fifty years here, the thought of uprooting these people and taking them away from their farm and the things they loved was terrible. Grandpa growing tea and vegetables, and Grandma growing her flowers. It was a cruel thing to do to them in their twilight years. But we had to get them ready to leave, anxious for their health and their safety. And my daughter, who was five, had to be ready to go to school. Al [the author's husband] had had a hemorrhage that winter, so we all had our personal grief as well.

The Farm Security Administration (FSA) told us that we should work until the very last moment. Yet we had to worry about selling our car and our refrigerator and about what we should do with our chickens and our pets. And we worried about trying to buy the right kind of things to get ready for a place we knew nothing about. We thought about camping. They said "camp," so we thought about going up in the mountains somewhere. I even bought boots thinking we would be up in the mountains where there might be snakes. Just ridiculous all the funny things we thought about!

In those days women didn't wear slacks much, but we all bought them, and we were running around trying to get ourselves ready. I was busy almost to the last day at the JACL office, sending the weekly bulletins and handling the personal problems of everybody. And I wrote to the President of the United States and the principal of the high school and the newspaper editors thanking them for whatever they did for us. I don't know if I was crazy to do this, but I felt that history was happening, and I felt that it was important to say good-bye in a proper way, speaking for the people who were leaving and trying to tell our friends that we were loyal Americans and that we were sorry that this was happening. We needed to say something, and that's what I did.

Evacuation Day

We left early in the morning on May 29, 1942. Two days earlier we sold our car for eight hundred dollars, which was just about giving it away. We also had to sell our refrigerator. But some wonderful friends came to ask if they could take care of some things we couldn't store. Mr. Lernard, a principal of a high school, took my piano, and his daughter took our dining table set, which was a wedding gift. They did that for us. Other things we had to sell, and still other things we had to crate. The Japanese community hall was declared the "federal reserve bank," a warehouse, and some of our things were stored there as well as in the Buddhist Church gymnasium. So people were bringing their stuff, crating it, stacking it up, and storing it. Some were working until the very last minute.

A few days earlier signs had been nailed to the telephone poles saying that we were to report to various spots. They told us to register as families. We had to report to the Elk Grove Masonic Building where we were given our family number, No. 2076. In the family I was *B* and my husband was *A*, and we were registered. We found out we were going to the Fresno Assembly Center.

The Community Is Split Up

It happened so suddenly to our community. You know, we grew up together, we went through the hardships of the Depression, and then finally things were picking up. People who had mortgages on their land were beginning to be able to make payments back to the bank. They were going to own the land that they had worked so hard to have. Then we had to evacuate. So there were still some people who owed some money on their property, and they lost the property because, of course, they couldn't make mortgage payments.

These were our people, and we loved them. We wept with them at their funerals and laughed with them and rejoiced at their weddings. And suddenly we found out that the community was going to be split up. The railroad track was one dividing line, and Florin Road the other dividing line. We were going to Fresno; the ones on the other side went to Manzanar; and the ones on the west side went to Tule. The ones on the west and north went to Pinedale and Poston. We never dreamed we would be separated—relatives and close friends, a community. The village people, we were just like brothers and sisters. We endured so much together and never dreamed we would be separated. Suddenly we found out we wouldn't be going to the same place. That was a traumatic disappointment and a great sadness for us. We were just tied up in knots, trying to cope with all of this happening at once and so fast. I can't understand why they had to do this. I don't know why they had to split us up.

We'll never forget the shock and grief and the sorrow on top of everything else that was happening to us. You know, every day we were supposed to pick berries, and that was important, because in those days we were barely making a living. We had to borrow ahead from companies and stores, and we had to borrow to buy groceries until we had our crop, and then we paid them. This is how we managed with the produce-shipping companies too. They loaned us money ahead, advanced it. So every day the berries being harvested and turned in was important to us so that we could get out from under a debt. We all tried very hard to pay our debts. If New Year's time came and we welcomed the new year with debts, it was a shame. That was an inherent part of the culture.

At the JACL office, we handled all kinds of problems. Let's say a big family came in. You can't split that family up. So we'd ask some smaller family that had signed up earlier for a different camp if they would be willing to go to Manzanar instead. Everybody got angry about things like that. We urged them to go somewhere else, and some of them didn't want to, because they were going to be separated from their friends and relatives. That was a tragic thing, and some of us were blamed for people being shipped to Manzanar. A lot of terrible things were said, and we were at each other's throats. The Japanese people were blaming me and the JACL for sending people every which way and keeping our personal friends together.

Tears

I don't know, we had been a very happy family. When we left, we swept our house and left it clean, because that's the way Japanese feel like leaving a place. I can just imagine everyone's emotions of grief and anger when they had to leave, when the military police (MPs) came and told them, "Get ready right now. You've got two hours to get ready to catch this train."

Early in the morning, Margaret and George File came after us in their car because we no longer had one to move our things. We had taken our luggage the day before on the pickup. We were very fortunate. Al had a very dear friend, Bob Fletcher, who was going to stay at our place and run our farm, our neighbor's farm, and Al's cousin's farm. So these three adjoining farms would be taken care of, at least the grape vineyards would be. Bob would stay at our place, and we left our dog with him. Nobody could take pets, and this was a sad thing for my daughter. There were tears everywhere; Grandma couldn't leave her flowers, and Grandpa looked at his grape vineyard. We urged him to get into the car and leave. I remember that sad morning when we realized suddenly that we wouldn't be free. It was such a clear, beautiful day, and I remember as we were driving, our tears. We saw the snow-clad Sierra Nevada mountains that we had loved to see so often, and I thought about God and about the prayer that we often prayed.

I remember one scene very clearly: on the train, we were told not to look out the window, but people were peeking out. After a long time on the train somebody said, "Oh, there's some Japanese standing over there." So we all took a peek, and we saw this dust, and rows and rows of barracks, and all these tan, brown Japanese people with their hair all bleached. They were all standing in a huddle looking at us, looking at this train going by. Then somebody on the train said, "Gee, that must be Japanese people in a camp." We didn't realize who they were before, but I saw how terrible it looked: the dust, no trees—just barracks and a bunch of people standing against the fence, looking out. Some children were hanging onto the fence like animals, and that was my first sight of the assembly center. I was so sad and discouraged looking at that, knowing that, before long, we would be inside too.

Chapter 4

Life in the Camps

Chapter Preface

O nce the Japanese evacuees were transferred from the assembly centers to permanent camps, many quickly set about trying to restore a semblance of normality to their lives. The task was made more difficult by the less-than-livable conditions many found at the relocation camps, most of which were located in the remote desert areas of Utah, Idaho, Colorado, Arizona, and California. Barracks-style housing had barely been completed and the rooms were furnished with nothing more than a few cots topped with straw-stuffed mattresses. Despite great hardship and a chronic lack of material, the internees quickly attempted to make their surroundings more habitable. They foraged for lumber to build furniture for their apartments, and partitions for increased privacy in the noisy and open barracks. The many professional gardeners and farmers among the internees transformed the barren wasteland around them into productive farms and lush green parks and gardens.

In addition to transforming the desert around them into a habitable place, the internees worked tirelessly to reestablish and maintain the important organizations and social institutions that had been a part of their lives on the West Coast. Churches and schools were quickly established and many of the relocation centers elected their own town councils. Movie theaters, Boy Scout troops, police and fire departments, baseball and softball leagues, hospitals, and camp newspapers all gave the internment camps the appearance of stable, small-town America. In many cases only the barbed wire fences and armed guards that surrounded the camps shattered the illusion.

From the Outrageous to the Tolerable

Jeanne Wakatsuki Houston and James D. Houston

> In the following essay, evacuee Jeanne Wakatsuki Houston
> describes how life at the Manzanar relocation camp in Cali-
> fornia gradually took on the semblance of life in other small
> towns in America. Manzanar residents slowly built livable
> homes and productive farms. Men who had been professional
> gardeners before relocation built lush parks and gardens. As
> the months turned into years, the accoutrements of other
> towns were becoming visible in Manzanar—schools,
> churches, Boy Scout troops, movie theaters, softball leagues,
> and police and fire departments. Only the barbed wire fences
> and armed guards distinguished Manzanar from other small
> towns, Houston recalls.

In Spanish, Manzanar means "apple orchard." Great
stretches of Owens Valley were once green with orchards
and alfalfa fields. It has been a desert ever since its water
started flowing south into Los Angeles, sometime during the
twenties. But a few rows of untended pear and apple trees
were still growing there when the camp opened, where a
shallow water table had kept them alive. In the spring of
1943 we moved to block 28, right up next to one of the old
pear orchards. That's where we stayed until the end of the
war, and those trees stand in my memory for the turning of
our life in camp, from the outrageous to the tolerable.

Papa pruned and cared for the nearest trees. Late that

summer we picked the fruit green and stored it in a root cellar he had dug under our new barracks. At night the wind through the leaves would sound like the surf had sounded in Ocean Park, and while drifting off to sleep I could almost imagine we were still living by the beach.

Mama had set up this move. Block 28 was also close to the camp hospital. For the most part, people lived there who had to have easy access to it. Mama's connection was her job as dietician. A whole half of one barracks had fallen empty when another family relocated. Mama hustled us in there almost before they'd snapped their suitcases shut.

The Congestion Is Eased

For all the pain it caused, the loyalty oath finally did speed up the relocation program. One result was a gradual easing of the congestion in the barracks. A shrewd househunter like Mama could set things up fairly comfortably—by Manzanar standards—if she kept her eyes open. But you had to move fast. As soon as the word got around that so-and-so had been cleared to leave, there would be a kind of tribal restlessness, a nervous rise in the level of neighborhood gossip as wives jockeyed for position to see who would get the empty cubicles.

In Block 28 we doubled our living space—four rooms for the twelve of us. Ray and Woody [the author's brothers] walled them with sheetrock. We had ceilings this time, and linoleum floors of solid maroon. You had three colors to choose from—maroon, black, and forest green—and there was plenty of it around by this time. Some families would vie with one another for the most elegant floor designs, obtaining a roll of each color from the supply shed, cutting it into diamonds, squares, or triangles, shining it with heating oil, then leaving their doors open so that passers-by could admire the handiwork.

Papa brought his still with him when we moved. He set it up behind the door, where he continued to brew his own sake [rice wine] and brandy. He wasn't drinking as much now, though. He spent a lot of time outdoors. Like many of the older Issei [first generation Japanese American] men, he didn't take a regular job in camp. He puttered. He had been working hard for thirty years and, bad as it was for him in some ways, camp did allow him time to dabble with hobbies he would never have found time for otherwise.

Once the first year's turmoil cooled down, the authorities started letting us outside the wire for recreation. Papa used to hike along the creeks that channeled down from the base of the Sierras. He brought back chunks of driftwood, and he would pass long hours sitting on the steps carving myrtle limbs into benches, table legs, and lamps, filling our rooms with bits of gnarled, polished furniture.

He hauled stones in off the desert and built a small rock garden outside our doorway, with succulents and a patch of moss. Near it he laid flat steppingstones leading to the stairs.

He also painted watercolors. Until this time I had not known he could paint. He loved to sketch the mountains. If anything made that country habitable it was the mountains themselves, purple when the sun dropped and so sharply etched in the morning light the granite dazzled almost more than the bright snow lacing it. The nearest peaks rose ten thousand feet higher than the valley floor, with Whitney, the highest, just off to the south. They were important for all of us, but especially for the Issei. Whitney reminded Papa of Fujiyama, that is, it gave him the same kind of spiritual sustenance. The tremendous beauty of those peaks was inspirational, as so many natural forms are to the Japanese (the rocks outside our doorway could be those mountains in miniature). They also represented those forces in nature, those powerful and inevitable forces that cannot be resisted, reminding a man that sometimes he must simply endure that which cannot be changed.

It Cannot Be Helped

Subdued, resigned, Papa's life—all our lives—took on a pattern that would hold for the duration of the war. Public shows of resentment pretty much spent themselves over the loyalty oath crises. *Shikata ga nai* [It Cannot Be Helped]

Self-Government

In an excerpt from Uprooted Americans: The Japanese Americans and the War Relocation Authority during World War II, *War Relocation Authority (WRA) director Dillon S. Myer writes that Japanese evacuees were encouraged to develop community governments. Following the guidelines laid down by the WRA, almost all of the relocation centers elected temporary councils.*

From the beginning the WRA staff felt that the evacuees should participate in governing their own communities to the extent possible under the mandate given to WRA and to the extent that the people could be encouraged to accept responsibilities that could properly be theirs. A division of opinion existed in the WRA only on the question as to whether we should await the development of an interest among the evacuees or whether we should proceed by laying down a framework of rules and letting the evacuees take it from there.

The general outlines of a policy were first set forth in an overall policy statement on May 29, 1942, and spelled out in

again became the motto, but under altered circumstances. What had to be endured was the climate, the confinement, the steady crumbling away of family life. But the camp itself had been made livable. The government provided for our physical needs. My parents and older brothers and sisters, like most of the internees, accepted their lot and did what they could to make the best of a bad situation. "We're here," Woody would say. "We're here, and there's no use moaning about it forever."

Gardens had sprung up everywhere, in the firebreaks, between the rows of barracks—rock gardens, vegetable gardens, cactus and flower gardens. People who lived in Owens Valley during the war still remember the flowers and lush greenery they could see from the highway as they drove past the main gate. The soil around Manzanar is alluvial and very rich. With water siphoned off from the Los Angeles-bound more detail on June 5. This tentative policy provided for a temporary council consisting of one representative elected from each block, an executive committee, and a judicial committee. The elected officers were to be American citizens, and all residents 16 years of age and over were eligible to vote.

This policy, however, was not long in effect. On August 13–15 a general WRA policy conference was held in San Francisco, involving all Washington and regional key staff members and the project directors who had been appointed up to that time. The policy on evacuee self-government was one of those revised as a result of this session. The revised policy issued on August 24, 1942, provided that all residents 18 years (rather than 16 as previously) and over would have voting rights. . . .

By the end of 1942 eight of the ten centers had elected temporary councils, and seven had established commissions to draw up charters for community government.

Dillon S. Myer, *Uprooted Americans: The Japanese Americans and the War Relocation Authority during World War II.* Tucson: University of Arizona Press, 1971.

aqueduct, a large farm was under cultivation just outside the camp, providing the mess halls with lettuce, corn, tomatoes, eggplant, string beans, horseradish, and cucumbers. Near Block 28 some of the men who had been professional gardeners built a small park, with mossy nooks, ponds, waterfalls and curved wooden bridges. Sometimes in the evenings we could walk down the raked gravel paths. You could face away from the barracks, look past a tiny rapids toward the darkening mountains, and for a while not be a prisoner at all. You could hang suspended in some odd, almost lovely land you could not escape from yet almost didn't want to leave.

Recreating Normality

As the months at Manzanar turned to years, it became a world unto itself, with its own logic and familiar ways. In time, staying there seemed far simpler than moving once again to another, unknown place. It was as if the war were forgotten, our reason for being there forgotten. The present, the little bit of busywork you had right in front of you, became the most urgent thing. In such a narrowed world, in order to survive, you learn to contain your rage and your despair, and you try to re-create, as well as you can, your normality, some sense of things continuing. The fact that America had accused us, or excluded us, or imprisoned us, or whatever it might be called, did not change the kind of world we wanted. Most of us were born in this country; we had no other models. Those parks and gardens lent it an oriental character, but in most ways it was a totally equipped American small town, complete with schools, churches, Boy Scouts, beauty parlors, neighborhood gossip, fire and police departments, glee clubs, softball leagues, Abbott and Costello movies, tennis courts, and traveling shows. (I still remember an Indian who turned up one Saturday billing himself as a Sioux chief, wearing bear claws and head feathers. In the firebreak he sang songs and danced his tribal dances

Japanese relocation camps gradually evolved into small towns as the evacuees tried to create a sense of normalcy. These detainees at a Boston camp stuff mattresses with straw.

while hundreds of us watched.)

In our family, while Papa puttered, Mama made her daily rounds to the mess halls, helping young mothers with their feeding, planning diets for the various ailments people suffered from. She wore a bright yellow, longbilled sun hat she had made herself and always kept stiffly starched. Afternoons I would see her coming from blocks away, heading home, her tiny figure warped by heat waves and that bonnet a yellow flower wavering in the glare.

Music

In their disagreement over serving the country, Woody and Papa had struck a kind of compromise. Papa talked him out of volunteering; Woody waited for the army to induct him. Meanwhile he clerked in the co-op general store. Kiyo [the author's brother], nearly thirteen by this time, looked forward to the heavy winds. They moved the sand around and uncovered obsidian arrowheads he could sell to old men in camp for fifty cents apiece. Ray, a few years older, played in the six-man touch football league, sometimes against Caucasian teams who would come in from Lone Pine or Independence. My sister Lillian was in high school and singing with a hillbilly band called The Sierra Stars—jeans, cowboy hats, two guitars, and a tub bass. And my oldest brother, Bill, led a dance band called The Jive Bombers—brass and rhythm, with cardboard fold-out music stands lettered J.B. Dances were held every weekend in one of the recreation halls. Bill played trumpet and took vocals on Glenn Miller arrangements of such tunes as *In the Mood*, *String of Pearls*, and *Don't Fence Me In*. He didn't sing *Don't Fence Me In* out of protest, as if trying quietly to mock the authorities. It just happened to be a hit song one year, and they all wanted to be an up-to-date American swing band. They would blast it out into recreation barracks full of bobby-soxed, jitterbugging couples:

Oh, give me land, lots of land
Under starry skies above,

Don't fence me in.
Let me ride through the wide
Open country that I love. . .

Pictures of the band, in their bow ties and jackets, appeared in the high school yearbook for 1943–1944, along with pictures of just about everything else in camp that year. It was called *Our World.* In its pages you see school kids with armloads of books, wearing cardigan sweaters and walking past rows of tarpapered shacks. You see chubby girl yell leaders, pompons flying as they leap with glee. You read about the school play, called *Growing Pains* ". . . the story of a typical American home, in this case that of the McIntyres. They see their boy and girl tossed into the normal awkward growing up stage, but can offer little assistance or direction in their turbulent course. . ." with Shoji Katayama as George McIntyre, Takudo Ando as Terry McIntyre, and Mrs. McIntyre played by Kazuko Nagai.

All the class pictures are in there, from the seventh grade through twelfth, with individual head shots of seniors, their names followed by the names of the high schools they would have graduated from on the outside: Theodore Roosevelt, Thomas Jefferson, Herbert Hoover, Sacred Heart. You see pretty girls on bicycles, chicken yards full of fat pullets, patients back-tilted in dental chairs, lines of laundry, and finally, two large blowups, the first of a high tower with a searchlight, against a Sierra backdrop, the next a two-page endsheet showing a wide path that curves among rows of elm trees. White stones border the path. Two dogs are following an old woman in gardening clothes as she strolls along. She is in the middle distance, small beneath the trees, beneath the snowy peaks. It is winter. All the elms are bare. The scene is both stark and comforting. This path leads toward one edge of camp, but the wire is out of sight, or out of focus. The tiny woman seems very much at ease. She and her tiny dogs seem almost swallowed by the landscape, or floating in it.

The Jewel of the Desert

Toyo Suyemoto Kawakami

> In October of 1942, Toyo Suyemoto Kawakami and her family
> arrived at Topaz, a relocation camp more familiarly known as
> "The Jewel of the Desert." Kawakami and the other evacuees
> wasted little time in trying to settle into a normal existence in
> the bleak and dusty surroundings of central Utah. Schools
> were developed and Kawakami served as an English teacher to
> both high school students and adults during her time as an
> internee. In addition to developing a camp newspaper, the resi-
> dents at Topaz opened a library in December 1942 and its col-
> lection grew extensively throughout its three year existence.
> According to Kawakami, Topaz began to feel like a commu-
> nity by the time the internment camps began to close in 1945.

In his book *The Immense Journey*, anthropologist Loren
Eiseley wrote: "It is a funny thing what the brain will do
with memories and how it will treasure them, and finally
bring them into odd juxtapositions with other things, as
though it wanted to make a design, or get some meaning out
of them, whether you want it or not, or even see it." So it is
that I have retained memories of the evacuation and internment that my people on the West Coast were subjected to in
1942. And so it was in September 1981 when I testified at
the Chicago hearings before the Commission on Wartime
Relocation and Internment of Civilians; I was made keenly
aware that the burden of memories, many sad and heavy, re-

mains in the minds of many.

My family—my parents, sisters, brothers, and not-quite-year-old son—and I arrived on October 3, 1942, at the Central Utah Relocation Project, known more familiarly as Topaz and dubbed "The Jewel of the Desert." We were among the last to leave the Tanforan Assembly Center, a former racetrack in San Bruno, California. We had traveled for three days on an old, rickety train to Delta, a farming town about seventeen miles from the camp and then by bus to Topaz.

As we stepped down from the bus, we were at the entry gate and I could see the earlier arrivals, among them my brother Bill, waiting to greet us. Bill had come in the advance work group of 214 volunteers who had reached Topaz on September 11. He was a bacteriologist, so he was included in the sanitary engineering crew. A small band of uniformed Boy Scouts stood in the hot sun and played on their brass instruments. When I heard them blare out the strains of "Hail to California," the song of my alma mater, I was suddenly homesick for Berkeley.

A Desolate Scene

Although we had grown accustomed to the barracks in Tanforan, this permanent camp was a strangely desolate scene of low, black, tar-paper buildings, row on row, through each block. The camp was only two-thirds finished, construction continuing even after people were moved into the unroofed barracks. The camp contained forty-two blocks, thirty-five of which were residential. All the blocks looked alike, so that later, weeks after we had settled in, camp residents would occasionally lose their sense of direction at night and wander into a barracks not their own, much to their embarrassment and that of the occupants.

With eleven members, our family was larger than most, so we were assigned to the two middle rooms of a barracks in Block 4. To go from one room to the other, we had to go outside. My brothers quickly opted to occupy one of these. Mother soon became tired of going out whenever she needed to see one of them, so one day Father cut a door-sized opening between them.

The first sight of our rooms was dismal—no furniture, unfinished walls and ceiling, a two-inch layer of fine dust on the floor and windowsills. We had to sweep out the dust and mop before we could bring our suitcases in. Army cots were delivered that night, giving us something to sit on. Eventually Father made a table and stools of varying heights from scrap lumber. Long afterwards I captured the initial impression of that moment in a sonnet.

Barracks Home

This is our barracks, squatting on the ground,
Tar-papered shack, partitioned into rooms
By sheetrock walls, transmitting every sound
Of neighbors' gossip or the sweep of brooms
The open door welcomes the refugees,
And now at last there is no need to roam
Afar: here space enlarges memories
Beyond the bounds of camp and this new home.

The floor is carpeted with dust, wind-borne
Dry alkali, patterned by insect feet.
What peace can such a place as this impart?
We can but sense, bewildered and forlorn,
That time, disrupted by the war from neat
Routines, must now adjust within the heart.

Adjusting to Restricted Living

As at Tanforan, we adjusted to restricted living and made the best of going to the mess hall at specified times for our meals; walking half a block to the latrine building in any weather; applying for the available jobs; opening schools, churches, and libraries; and trying to lead as normal an existence as possible. Several of my sisters and brothers applied for work at the hospital and I for teaching in the camp high school and in the adult education division. Since education is traditionally respected among the Japanese, two nursery schools were established for preschool children and

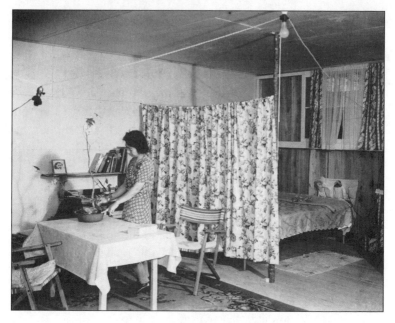

Internment camp barracks were dismal and dirty. Evacuees cleaned and furnished them as best they could with what few belonging they brought with them and with furniture made from whatever scrap lumber could be found.

elementary and high schools for the older children.

I taught high school English and Latin during the day and basic English to Issei [first generation Japanese American] and Kibei [American-born Japanese who were educated in Japan] students in the evening. The high school students were Americanized in their speech, manners, and attitudes, whereas the adults were almost deferential towards me as their teacher, although I was as young as some of their children.

I found teaching adult education rewarding. The classes in basic English were on three levels: the beginning group, whose comprehension of English was about that of the second grade; the intermediate, whose reading skill approximated that of the fourth grade; and the advanced, about the seventh grade. Among the advanced were some Kibei, who had been born in the United States, but were sent to Japan to live with relatives during their childhood. For one semester I taught an evening extension course in creative writing and had college-level Nisei [second generation Japanese American] students, several from Hawaii, and one Englishwoman from Yorkshire in camp because of her half-Japanese son.

The beginning adult students were mainly the Issei, a few of them the parents of my high school pupils. I truly enjoyed their presence in my classes, and my fellow teachers in the adult education division felt the same about their groups. The Issei's reason for learning English, so they stated, was to better adapt to the "outside" when war was over and to understand their children, whose values sometimes conflicted with theirs. These adult students often had difficulty with pronunciation, providing hilarious moments for all of us. They would even pun on some words. By saying "So Utah!" and prolonging the vowels, they could imply in Japanese, "So it is said!" The *l* and *r*, the *v* and *b*, and *th* were difficult for them, yet they did practice earnestly. I would hear suppressed giggling among the women when *salary* and *celery* came out sounding the same as *sa-ra-ri* or when *very* was enunciated as *berry*. Then they would apologize for their mistakes. Many a time as I faced them in the classroom, I felt humbled that here I was teaching them when I myself should have been their pupil learning from them of their enduring patience, reticent affection, and wise sense of humor.

The Topaz Public Library

After teaching for almost two years, I was transferred to work in the public library. The Topaz Public Library originated when 5,000 books, gifts from personal friends and from California schools, colleges, and public libraries had been assembled and shipped to Utah. Topaz residents donated additional books and magazines until the library's holdings numbered almost 7,000 books and several thousand issues of periodicals. The public library was dependent upon minimal fines and donations to purchase needed supplies and books. From this meager income we started a rental collection of current best-sellers. A five cents per week rental charge and a quick turnover enabled us to order more new titles.

There were delays in getting the roof of the library tarred, the cast-iron stoves installed for heating, and the walls and ceilings sheetrocked for insulation. The climate in Utah sometimes necessitated closing the library in the afternoon because of the bitter cold.

An Enthusiastic Response

The library opened on December 1, 1942, and the next day presented a concert of classical recordings. Audience response was so enthusiastic that concerts were given every Wednesday. Program notes, with information about the selections, composers, and the following week's program, were mimeographed for those attending the concerts. Library notes and book reviews appeared in the *Topaz Times*, the camp newspaper, which was also mimeographed. The library was later moved to another barracks in Block 16. Half the building space, totaling 20 by 100 feet, contained adult fiction and nonfiction and the other half, the children's section and periodicals. One small end room was used for bookbinding and mending, the other end for an office and cataloging; mess-hall tables, with attached benches, filled the reading room.

A rotating collection of selected titles was borrowed from the Salt Lake County Library at Midvale and shelved in a special section, adding variety to the overall collection. In January 1943, college libraries of Utah and the University of California at Berkeley granted interlibrary loan services, extending the scope of the public library considerably.

Towards the end of February 1943, gravel was laid for a pathway from the unpaved road to the library so people could come to the building without slipping in mud or slush. When attendance reached about 450 persons each day, the library was kept open in the evenings. To brief the residents on world news, the reports division of the camp administration sent weekly news-maps for posting on the library bulletin board. Outside newspapers were received on subscription, among them the *Oakland Tribune* and the *San Francisco Chronicle* for the many Bay Area residents in camp.

In time, Relocation Authority funding increased the number of magazine subscriptions from fourteen to fifty-two. The rental collection also grew, and bright covers from new books decorated the library walls. Since the rental books had been made possible from fees paid by the camp people, they were sold just before the library closed, at greatly reduced prices, to benefit the Topaz Scholarship Fund and help high school students to relocate.

Starting Over

As 1945 turned towards autumn, the relocation camps began to close and people left to start life over on the outside. In Topaz, as more residents left and the blocks emptied, I thought wonderingly of this place, a community created by government order and now dispersed. Conjecture and wonderment remained long after my family had moved to Cincinnati, and still more time had to pass before I could write farewell to our internment camp.

Topaz, Utah

The desert must have claimed its own
Now that the wayfarers are gone,
And silence has replaced voices
Except for intermittent noises,
Like windy footsteps through the dust,
Or gliding of a snake that must
Escape the sun, or sage rustling.
Or soft brush of a quickened wing
Against the air.—Stillness is change
For this abandoned place, where strange
And foreign tongues had routed peace
Until the refugees' release
Restored calm to the wilderness,
And prairie dogs no longer fear
When shadows shift and disappear.
The crows fly straight through settling dusk,
The desert like an empty husk,
Holding the small swift sounds that run
To cover when the day is done.

Thus it was, as I wrote my friend Mine Okubo, the Nisei artist, now of New York, who recorded our stay at Tanforan and Topaz with her sketches in her book *Citizen 13660*; I have shared with you some camp memories:

> Camp Memories
> I have dredged up
> Hard fragments lost I
> thought, in years
> Of whirlwind dust.
>
> Exposed to light,
> Silently rough
> And broken shards
> Confront belief.

Life at Gila

Anonymous

> This account of life at the Gila relocation camp in Arizona was
> given by a Japanese American watch repairman from central
> California who was initially sent to the assembly center at
> Tulare, near Fresno. The conditions found by the evacuees
> upon their arrival at Gila were primitive. Families were sup-
> plied nothing more than a bare room and a few cots to sleep
> on. As the internees settled in, however, they began to build
> livable homes in the dusty surroundings of the Arizona desert.
> Many settled into a day-to-day routine—working, going to
> school, attending church services—that was similar to life
> before evacuation. The following essay is excerpted from an
> interview contained in *The Salvage,* a book compiled by
> Dorothy Swaine Thomas for the University of California Japa-
> nese American Evacuation and Resettlement Study (JERS).

When it was announced that we were going to be sent
to Gila, I didn't have any great reaction one way or
the other. There wasn't any way out of the situation, since
we were not given any alternatives. The Japanese people began to pass around all sorts of rumors about the snakes,
scorpions, and heat in Arizona, and a lot of people in my
block made a petition to ask the Army if they could not remain at Tulare [an assembly center near Fresno, California].
All of us wanted to stay in Tulare and we dreaded the idea
of going to Gila. But when the first group started to leave,
the people all wanted to go there so that they could stick together as one group.

Excerpted from an anonymous account of life in the Gila relocation camp, quoted in *The
Salvage,* by Dorothy Swaine Thomas (Berkeley & Los Angeles: University of California
Press, 1952).

I was really disgusted when I got to Gila. It was nothing but a desert and everything was so dusty. The camp looked so primitive and we felt pretty well cut off from everything. Everything was confusion when we arrived. The baggage lot was an empty block which was covered with dust so that all of our clothes in the bags were practically ruined. This dust was so soft that we would sink in with every step. We had no choice in housing, as other Japanese were coming in every day. It got so crowded that a lot of families had to double up. Fortunately my wife and family got a separate apartment but it was located in one of the hottest spots in camp. We figured that we would be in Gila permanently for the duration, so we began to fix our apartment up much better than we had at Tulare. I stole lumber along with other people so that I could build the benches and table. My wife ordered material for curtains, awning for the windows, and other things like that, in order to make living more comfortable for us. I purchased a cooler from Sears Roebuck, so that we would not roast to death. I was fortunate in being able to buy a new one for less than $30. After Sears Roebuck ran out of the coolers, the people in camp were paying $70 and $80 for a fan. I found out that some Caucasians in Arizona had bought the supply of coolers out. A man came to camp in a truck loaded with these coolers and he sold the identical fan that I had for $30 to other people for $70 and $80. Later on the administration found out about this and they made the man give a refund of $30 to $40 for each fan, according to the ceiling price. The only trouble was that a lot of the families did not save their receipts, so that they were out of luck.

Making a Home

We didn't have any privacy at all in our apartment, and I did not think this was so good for our children. I bought some sheeting material and I was able to partition our room up into 2 small bedrooms and a living room. We ordered quite a few things from the mail order company in order to complete our household. We also sent for some more of our clothing and other necessities from back home. I was expecting to get a whole box of canned goods from my former grocery store but somebody switched the boxes and we were sent a case of noodles instead. That was the last thing we wanted because we were getting plenty of noodles in camp. I also sent for my electric hot-plate so that we could cook little snacks at home for the children and also for company.

With the left-over lumber I built a nice big porch in the front of our apartment so that we could sit out there during the hot evenings. Later on we put in a lawn. We had some trouble with our next door neighbor because he infringed upon our property and this burnt my wife up, because she wanted the space for a garden. Some people in camp were certainly greedy and they wanted everything for themselves.

After everything was fixed up at home, I went to look for a job. Again, I had some difficulty in finding work as the good jobs were monopolized by the first-comers. The employment officer finally told me that there was an opening for a typewriter repair man. There weren't too many typewriters in camp so I wasn't very busy.

A little later the adult education department started to look for a radio instructor. I coöperated with them, so I began to teach radio about three evenings a week besides fixing the typewriters. I had a nice crowd of enthusiastic boys who were interested in learning about radios, so that I enjoyed this experience. I did this combination of work until the end of the semester in January, 1943.

Setting Up Shop

After that I had an opportunity to become the manager of the repair department for the Community Enterprises. I had quite a difficult time getting it organized. My first job was to get the watch-repair shop started. It took me a long time to find the right man to do this work. We had to build all of the benches and fix up the shop ourselves. I could only find one man in camp with his watch-repairing tools, so I had to give him the job. Later I sent back home for some of my watch-repairing tools and I loaned this equipment to Community Enterprises. The dust and heat in camp had ruined many a watch so that we got more work than we could handle in the watch shop. After this shop became successful, I began to fix up a radio repair shop in the same room. Business was very brisk and we really earned our $19 a month.

There were many evacuees who brought their radios to my apartment to get fixed. I never charged them anything for this work but sometimes they insisted on giving me small tips. It would have taken them 3 times as long to get their radio fixed through the radio shop, so I felt justified in taking these tips. I usually gave it all to my three children. Before the war I used to make more in one day than I did in the whole month in camp for doing the same work.

About this time I got an idea that I wanted to make a little quick money, so I thought I would go to the camouflage net factory for a while. I made quite a bit of money compared to the War Relocation Authority (WRA) wages, but a lot of it was deducted for the net trust fund and taxes. I made about $212 in all for the 15 days of work. Then they started to close up the factory because the net contract with the Army was ended. After this job, I got a job as an electrician for the camp. I had to take care of the electrical troubles for the whole center. We even had to repair the power line occasionally. It was something a little different for me and I learned quite a bit. Some of the Issei [first generation Japanese Americans] wanted me to put in shortwave systems for them but I refused to do this. I know that there were a few short waves in camp, but I never located them myself.

My social life in Gila was not quite as interesting or as varied as my work. I made some new friends and we spent most of our evenings playing cards. I also went to a number of dances and private parties with my wife. The social life in Gila was about the same as it was in Tulare.

A Routine Existence

Life at Gila became pretty routine after being there for some months. I had to go to church a few times as I took care of the sound system for the Christian Church. My wife sent the children to the Buddhist Church because she had been brought up as a Buddhist. I didn't mind it at all because I didn't particularly believe in any religion. Back home we didn't have a Buddhist Church in town. My wife wanted her children to know a little bit about her religion so I couldn't object about that. I didn't think it would influence my children's thinking to more Japanese ways anyway. I really didn't know what they taught in the Buddhist Church, but I did not think it was harmful to my children while in camp as long as the religion taught them to be good and honest.

As evacuees settled into interment camps, schools such as this one in Poston, Arizona, were organized so that children could continue their education.

Two of my older girls were going to school in camp and the youngest was in kindergarten. I realized that my children wouldn't get as good an education as on the outside and that bothered my wife and myself at times. We tried to train our children to behave properly in all aspects of living because there was so much of a tendency for young children in camp to go unsupervised. I also thought at times that it was too bad that my children did not have the Caucasian contacts in the regular school, but I knew that it would not be for all the time. I didn't want my children to grow up with the feeling of inferiority to the white people.

My youngest girl always used to ask us to go back to our white house in our home town and it was difficult to answer her. We just had to tell her that some day we would go back. It was hard when they asked questions like this. Sometimes the children asked my wife why we were moved from California and it was hard to explain to them. Once my oldest daughter wanted to know if we were going to be sent to Japan. These were the most difficult times for me and I couldn't answer them definitely except to say that some day we would all go back to California to the life we had before. I never liked it when these "why" questions were asked as I didn't know what to say. We would just tell the children the news of our home town when we got letters from friends.

I think my wife had a great deal of difficulty in adjusting herself to the condition of camp life for a long time as the housekeeping facilities were not what she had been used to. But she did manage to mix with the people much easier than I did since her mother was there and she knew more of the people from before.

The Loyalty Question

The registration for the Army in February, 1943, was about the only thing which broke the routine of life in camp. It was too easy to slip into the routine life there and forget about the outside. The registration didn't affect me very much although a lot of people were greatly disturbed about it. I didn't go to any of those public meetings as there was no question about how I would register. I answered "yes" to both 27 and 28 and my wife did the same thing.[1]

The registration did make me stop to think that there was a great deal of resentment against the government by the people in camp. There were a few pro-Japan people there and they influenced a lot of the people who would have answered "yes" if they had not been so aroused by these agitators. I didn't know who all the pro-Japan individuals were, but I was acquainted with a couple of them. I talked to them a few times, but I found that it was no use arguing with them, as they were stubborn and set in their ways of thinking. I tried to keep away from them as much as possible after I found out their type of thinking. A lot of the Kibei [American-born Japanese who had been educated in Japan] signed up for a segregation camp because they felt they had been kicked out of the United States Army after the war started, and they said they were not wanted here anymore.

Many of the Issei who went to Tule Lake [a segregation camp for disloyal Japanese] were rather bitter against the United States because they had lost their life earnings and they did not see a chance for themselves in this country any more. They thought that their children would have more of a chance to be accepted as equals in Japan. They thought that Japan wanted them to go back there. My opinion was that they were doing wrong and they were being misled. I thought that they would have even less of a chance to get back on their feet in Japan. I felt sorry for the Nisei [second generation Japanese American] children whose parents signed up for repatriation, as I knew that they would have a difficult time ever getting adjusted to life in Japan, when and if they are ever sent back.

Note

1. Question 27 on the registration form asked: "Are you willing to serve in the Armed Forces of the United States on combat duty, wherever ordered?" Women were asked if they would join the Women's Army Corps (WACS) or the Army Nurses Corps. Question 28 asked: "Would you swear unqualified allegiance to the United States of America and faithfully defend the United States from any or all attack by foreign or domestic forces, and foreswear any form of allegiance or obedience to the Japanese emperor, or any other foreign government, power, or organization?"

Keeping the Family Together at Minidoka

Helen Murao

> In the following essay, evacuee Helen Murao recalls the diffi-
> culty of maintaining a normal family life during the Japanese
> American relocation. Among a sizeable population of Japa-
> nese for the first time, Murao, a fifteen-year-old orphan when
> she was evacuated from Portland, Oregon, took on the
> responsibility of raising her two younger brothers. When they
> were transferred to the relocation camp at Minidoka, Idaho,
> Murao, determined to maintain the cohesiveness of the family
> unit, intensively supervised her brothers' lives while working
> a job and trying to finish high school.

I was born in Portland, Oregon, in 1926. . . . I had gotten
through my sophomore year in high school when evacuation came about. I did a year of high school, such as it was,
in camp and then finished up in Madison, Wisconsin.

My parents died within three years of each other in the
mid-thirties, my mother dying first. I was still in grammar
school when that happened, and we became wards of the
state. I had an older sister, Mary, who died after this, but she
was not at home, so I was the oldest of the three of us, me
and my two younger brothers. The Japanese community was
very fearful and very reluctant to take us into their homes
because Mary had had tuberculosis, and there was nothing
more fearful to them than that disease. So they did not offer
their homes to us—even our very close family friends. It

Excerpted from "Minidoka," by Helen Murao, in *And Justice for All: An Oral History of
the Japanese American Detention Camps*, by John Tateishi. Copyright ©1984 by John
Tateishi. Reprinted by permission of the University of Washington Press.

was with Caucasian people that we made our homes. My two brothers were with Japanese families at the time of evacuation, but they were Japanese who were not friends of my parents. They had been asked by the members of the church, so they were doing it as a charitable thing, the Christian thing to do. It was not out of friendship. During those years it was very hard for me to come to grips with the realization that the Japanese people forsook us. They just didn't want to have anything to do with us. Just out of fear for their health.

At the time that my father died, our next-door neighbors were a very young Caucasian couple, who had come from Nebraska and had never seen Orientals in their life. My dad had helped them when they came by giving them fuel for the furnace and kind of helping them out. So that when my dad died very unexpectedly, this couple, without a moment's thought, took the three of us into their home. And they couldn't afford it—they didn't have room or anything. But they did it just as an act of kindness. And we lived with them for the better part of a year in a two-bedroom house, until their younger child got pneumonia, and they just couldn't do it anymore. I was to have stayed with them, and the two boys were to go to other homes. . . .

Evacuation

Well, my sister died April 24, which was like a week before evacuation. We were evacuated from Portland May 5, 1942. Before she died, when she was still out of the hospital, the plan was for her to go with the boys. She was going to take the two boys, and I was going to stay with this Caucasian family. I was very attached to this family because. . . I don't know, I think there was an affection or a show of affection or a sense of belonging that I just hadn't had. It was very important for me to keep this. I think Mary sensed this, and so she said, "You stay there," and she would evacuate with the two boys. And then she had her relapse and went to the hospital, and . . . she died. So, within a week's time, I had to make a very serious decision. That was, to go in my sister's place. When we had to go on the fifth of May, I evacuated with my two brothers. . . .

I made my own decision. Nobody even approached me about it. I made my decision to go into camp with the two boys. At that point, as loving as my foster parents were, I did not think that they were good for me, and I think it's a good thing that I did not continue living with them. But I didn't know it at the time. They took me to the Portland Assembly Center and said good-bye to me. My foster mother had helped me pack, and we packed camp clothes, summer-camp clothes. You know how you pack shorts and tennis shoes and things like this. And I packed for maybe three weeks and thought this is only for a while, I'll be back. So I left school clothes, good clothes, cold-weather clothes and things like this, and books. I just took enough necessities for three weeks, thinking I surely would be back. She let me feel this way; she let me believe this way and let me prepare this way and took me to camp.

My First Experience Among Japanese People

This was the first experience I'd ever had with living among Japanese people. Our home had been in the north part of Portland where we were the only Japanese family. So that, as children, we went to school as the only Japanese family in school, and our peer associations were not with Japanese people at all, so this was my first experience among Japanese people.

There was an overwhelming, confusing feeling, and it was just all negative—all bad feelings that I had. Not only the country having done this—causing us to have to be evacuated—but the Japanese people having done this to us. So I really was a very unhappy, bitter child, and I really entertained, at fleeting moments, some feelings that maybe I'd be better off if, you know, I tried to . . . I felt it might be a solution if I just did away with my brothers' and my own life. I thought that. I entertained that as a possibility, as a solution, and then abandoned it. But I thought this because it was so black for me at one point, you know. If your country is doing this to you, and if your people are doing this to you . . . I just couldn't see a way out of a big black hole. But I gave that idea up, obviously.

We spent the summer, through the end of August 1942 when we were evacuated into Idaho, in the Portland Assembly Center, which had been where they had stock shows. I remembered that from the time my parents took us to things like county fairs and stock shows. This was the county-fair grounds. All the places were very familiar to me as a child, and I recognized the place where we were assigned as the pavilion where they kept animals. They had these one by six's or one by nine's, however large those boards are, with big knotholes, just over the pens. It was a huge pavilion with twelve-foot-high plywood walls and with curtains as doors. Row after row after row of these. My two brothers and I were assigned to one of these. We had cots, and a curtain to cover the door, and our belongings. You've heard it all before. We ate in the community mess hall. We were given salt tablets because the weather was so hot. . . .

An Overwhelming Experience

When I went into camp I was just overwhelmed with the numbers of Nisei [second generation Japanese American] boys and girls and everybody. But also I would remember taking walks with my sister's boyfriend and telling him how I felt about how angry I was at the Japanese people, at the world, people in general, the country in general, the war, the everything. And that I wanted to have nothing to do with the Japanese people. And he would say, yes, but so-and-so wants a date with you. And I'd say, that's terrific, but I don't want to have anything to do with him, not at all. And he would say, now you think about it. You may feel different, but you aren't different. You're one of us. Like it or not, you are here. You chose to come here. Face it and live with it.

That summer I had this sorting out and coming to terms with my own self and my own life. It was not an easy time. When my brothers and I got to the Portland Assembly Center there were no persons, no agency, no group there to counsel not only me but anybody. No social workers, no social-service agency of any kind. There was an infirmary for cuts and bruises, but nothing else. I know, because I went seeking help one day when I can't tell you how low I felt. If a kid fifteen years old could even consider suicide, you know that she's got to be awfully unhappy. I went seeking some help and was directed by someone in charge to the infirmary. That's not what I needed.

There was nobody to give me any kind of emotional support of any sort—no Caucasians or Japanese personnel. I guess that this probably was the worst experience of my life, the hardest period of my life. I somehow got it all in my mind that it was the United States government, and it was this country, and it was the Japanese people—everybody was really out to do this to us. At that point, even if it hadn't been for the war, I might have felt this way. But I think that evacuation just heightened it all because it was just heaping one indignity after another onto me. It was just almost more than I could handle, it really was.

I'm Going to Prevail

By Labor Day 1942, when we were to be moved inland to Idaho, I guess I was beginning to feel that I had no choice. I had to quit being so angry and to quit being so hateful. I had a job to do with my brothers, and I ran them like a drill sergeant, and people who met me in those years smile and laugh and talk about it now; they say, "Helen ran those boys like she was a drill sergeant." I wouldn't let them be out after nine o'clock, I made them go to school, I made them study, I made them . . . you know. I had them help me scrub their clothes so that they would be clean. Then somewhere during that time I came to feel, well, we're going to show these people. We're going to show the world. They are not going to do this to me; nobody is going to make me feel this miserable. The United States government may have made me leave my home, but they're going to be sorry. You know what I mean; I came around to feeling that nobody's going to do this to me. *I'm going to prevail, my will is going to prevail, my own life will prevail.* I'm not going to kill myself, I'm going to prevail.

I made up my mind that my two brothers and I would show everybody. We were orphans, yes; we had come from an unhealthy family, a tubercular family, and we were like pariahs, but I made up my mind, and I told my brothers that we will excel, and we will be better than anybody so that they'll be sorry. Not that they would be proud of us, but they would be sorry, the whole world would be sorry that they did this to us. It was not a healthy attitude on my part.

At Idaho's Minidoka we were assigned our barracks. Well, the end rooms of the barracks were the small rooms, quite small, the smallest. We were given one of those. It was usually for two people, but since we were kids and we didn't take up so much space, three of us were put in one of those end barracks. But I do remember managing to get a bed by using feminine wiles because the guys in camp were teenagers, and they were running up and down the block saying, "There's one over there," and "There's a good one over here." They were pegging the families that were coming in that had—you know—good-looking girls. They came running up to me, ran in and looked, and they saw that it was me, that there were no parents around. They asked how many beds? The camp was giving out pillow ticking that you filled with straw, and cots. The old and the infirm got beds with mattresses, and the younger people got cots and pillow ticking. I managed to finagle a real bed with a real mattress from these guys. I thought that was pretty neat. That's all we had, that's absolutely all we had.

I had no skills, and I did not want to work as a waitress. So, I lied and said I could type, and I worked in a steno pool. Well, the fellow watched me and he knew damned well I couldn't type. I couldn't. But, again, I used whatever I could muster up and batted my eyelashes and said I would be a hard worker. He let me stay, but not because of any typing expertise, he just let me do that. So I had a job for which I was paid. A stenographic job was sixteen dollars a month, and I was part-time, so I got eight dollars a month.

I was still in high school, so I had to go to class. My two brothers had to go too, and I lied a lot because I didn't want to go. I would stay at home, because the hot water in the mess hall and in the laundry rooms was available in the morning. I would scrub my brothers' blue jeans and their clothes on a washboard and try to wring them out and also launder our sheets in the morning. Then I would write a note saying, "Please excuse Helen for being absent, she was busy." And then I'd sign it, and the teacher would accept it. I still managed to get good grades. But I never, never, was in class. I insisted that my two brothers and I eat together in the mess hall as a family unit. I insisted that we have grace before meals. And I insisted that they be in our room at eight o'clock at night. Not because I wanted to see them but because I thought that's what we should do as a family unit—we should be together, spend our time together, and live as a family group—and I tried in all the really childish ways to maintain us that way. It's incredible, as I think about it now, how we did it; but we lived as a family unit. I don't know what gave me the strength to do it, but I can't help but feel that those early years with my parents must have given it to me. It must have been that, because that year and a half from evacuation until the time when I left camp were terribly hard times. Not only for me emotionally, but just keeping body and soul together. And that whole time we had absolutely no money, absolutely no financial support. No emotional support either. No adult nurturing of any kind. The people were so wrapped up in their own misery in camp, in their own unhappiness, in their own problems, which is only to be expected, that nobody had anything to give to anybody else. It didn't occur to them that maybe we were needy in other ways.

Freedom

We got out of camp because we had a sponsor. It was in August 1943. The same woman who helped me plan my sister's funeral worked for the Baptist Home Mission Society. I wrote to her, and I said it was imperative that I get out immediately. I said, "Will you find me a place?" And, again, there's something that's marvelous about being young and ignorant; you just ask and somehow things materialize. She had access to homes throughout the country willing to take students. She sent me a list of several, and one of them was a family, a Presbyterian minister and his family, in Madison, Wisconsin. They wanted an evacuee. I didn't stop to think whether that was going to be all right or not; it just meant getting out. So I went. They were a terrific family. When I came out of camp, they gave me the support that I really sorely needed, and they have been friends ever since.

I felt wonderful the day I left camp. We took a bus to the railroad siding and then stopped someplace to transfer, and I went in and bought a Coke, a nickel Coke. It wasn't the Coke, but what it represented—that I was free to buy it, that feeling was so intense. You can get maudlin, sentimental about freedom; but if you've been deprived of it, it's very significant. When I ran in there as a teenager to buy that Coke, it was the freedom to buy it, the freedom to run out and do it.

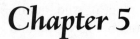

Chapter 5

Freedom

Chapter Preface

As U.S. and Allied forces closed in on victory in the Pacific, restrictions on Japanese Americans were lifted. On December 17, 1944, Major General Henry C. Pratt, acting commander of the Western Defense Command (General DeWitt had been dismissed in late 1943), issued Public Proclamation Number Twenty-one, which restored the rights of evacuees to return to their former homes. The next day, internment was officially brought to an end when the Supreme Court ruled in favor of Mitsuye Endo, an internee who in 1942 filed a writ of habeas corpus, compelling the government to either release her or provide just cause as to why she should be interned. In ruling in favor of Endo, the Court stated that the government could not detain loyal citizens without just cause. Since no evidence of disloyalty had been presented against Japanese Americans, they were free to go.

Though the West Coast was off-limits to the Japanese until 1944, the War Relocation Authority (WRA) had permitted certain groups of evacuees to leave the camps as early as October 1942. Japanese Americans who applied to college or found work outside of the camps were allowed to resettle in the East and Midwest. Once the relocation camps started to close, some family members followed loved ones who had established new lives in these areas. Many Japanese Americans, however, missed the mild climate of their old homes on the West Coast. One former internee wrote, "We don't have a home to go back to and will have to stay at the hostel or at a hotel until we can find something else. I want to go back to Tacoma [Washington] where I lived for a long time." Though they had to begin their lives anew with virtually nothing, many decided to return to the Pacific coast.

Putting the Pieces Back Together

Yoshiko Uchida

In the following essay, Yoshiko Uchida describes her family's
attempt to piece together their lives upon their release from
the Topaz relocation center in Utah. Uchida, like many Nisei,
or second generation Japanese Americans, moved east to
attend school and find work when she was released from custody. As a consequence, her parents moved east as well. Yet
like many Issei, or first generation Japanese immigrants,
Uchida's parents missed the mild climate of their old home
on the Pacific coast and soon moved back. With stoic composure and patient discipline, and with minimal reimbursement
from the government, Uchida describes how Japanese Americans quietly set about rebuilding their lives in the west.

A Japanese American recently asked me how the fourth
generation Japanese Americans could be proud of their
heritage when their grandparents and great-grandparents had
been incarcerated in concentration camps. I was stunned by
the question, for quite the contrary, I think they should be
proud of the way in which their grandparents survived that
shattering ordeal. It is our country that should be ashamed
of what it did, not the Japanese Americans for having been
its victims.

Although some Issei were shattered and broken by the experience, those I knew and observed personally, endured the
hardship of the evacuation with dignity, stoic composure,

Excerpted from *Desert Exile: The Uprooting of a Japanese American Family*, by Yoshiko
Uchida (Seattle: University of Washington Press, 1982). Copyright ©1982 by Yoshiko
Uchida. Reprinted by permission of The Bancroft Library of the University of California,
Berkeley.

disciplined patience, and an amazing resiliency of spirit. I think they displayed a level of strength, grace, and courage that is truly remarkable.

Like many other Issei, my parents made the best of an intolerable situation. Throughout their internment they maintained the values and faith that sustained them all their lives. They continued to be the productive, caring human beings they had always been, and they continued always to have hope in the future. They helped my sister and me channel our anger and frustration into an effort to get out of camp and get on with our education and our lives. They didn't want us to lose our sense of purpose, and I am grateful they didn't nurture in us the kind of soul-decaying bitterness that would have robbed us of energy and destroyed us as human beings. Our anger was cathartic, but bitterness would have been self-destructive.

Survival

Perhaps I survived the uprooting and incarceration because my Issei parents taught me to endure. Perhaps I survived because at the time I believed I was taking the only viable path and believed what I was doing was right. Looking back now, I think the survival of the Japanese through those tragic, heartbreaking days was a triumph of the human spirit. And I hope future generations of Japanese Americans, remembering that, will never feel stigmatized by the incarceration of the Issei and Nisei.

From the concentration camps the Nisei went out to all parts of the United States, some to schools and others to seek employment. They were accepted with warmth and concern by some Americans, but treated with contempt and hatred by others.

The white friends to whom I went from Topaz accepted me without hesitation into the warmth of their family circle. But there were others, such as the conductor on the train I rode to Northampton, Massachusetts. "You'd better not be a Jap," he threatened as he took my ticket, "because if you are, I'll throw you off the train."

I left Topaz determined to work hard and prove I was as

Stockton Fairgrounds and Race Track was converted into a temporary detention center during the war. Japanese Americans were held here prior to being transferred to one of ten internment camps.

loyal as any other American. I felt a tremendous sense of responsibility to make good, not just for myself, but for all Japanese Americans. I felt I was representing all the Nisei, and it was sometimes an awesome burden to bear.

When the war was over, the brilliant record of the highly decorated Nisei combat teams, and favorable comments of the GIs returning from Japan, helped alleviate to some degree the hatred directed against the Japanese Americans during the war. Although racism had by no means been eliminated, new fields of employment, previously closed, gradually opened up for many Nisei. In time they were also able to purchase and rent homes without being restricted to ghetto areas as the Issei had been.

Life in the East

The Issei's productive years were now coming to an end, and it was time for the Nisei to take care of their parents. My own parents came east from Salt Lake City to live with my sister and me. We spent a year in Philadelphia where I taught in a small Quaker school and was accepted with warmth by the children, their parents, and my colleagues. My father found work in the shipping department of a church board and became one of their best packers.

We eventually moved to New York City, where my sister became a teacher in a private nursery school and I worked as a secretary. My father, however, had difficulty finding work. A friend found a job for him in a factory painting flowers on glassware, but in spite of his enthusiasm in this totally unfamiliar milieu, he was dismissed after a few days because he lacked the proper skills. It was the first time in his entire life that he had been dismissed from a job, but with his usual sense of humor, he recounted the experience to his friends with amusement rather than rancor.

Like most Issei, my parents missed the mild climate of California and found it depressing to be confined in our dark three-room apartment. My father, especially, longed for a house and a garden where he could again enjoy growing things. My parents finally returned to California and lived for a time in two small rooms of "the Back House" at our old Japanese church in Oakland, which had been converted, as were several other Japanese churches, into a temporary hostel for returning Japanese Americans.

My father had lost virtually all of his retirement benefits at the now defunct Mitsui and Company, but he had not lost his spirit or vitality. He was determined and eager to begin a new life, and my mother, although her health was deteriorating, was ready to begin with him.

In May 1949 my father filed three "Claims for Damage to or Loss of Real or Personal Property by a Person of Japanese Ancestry" in the names of my mother, my sister, and myself, making sure that the total amount did not exceed the limit, which he understood to be $2,500. My claim for my personal belongings and expenses related to the evacuation came to $1,037, and in June 1952 I was awarded the sum of $386.25, the bulk of which I sent to my parents. Although the Japanese Americans suffered losses estimated by the Federal Reserve Bank to have been roughly $400 million, the average award for some 23,000 claimants was only $440.

Making a New Life in California

Following his return to California, my father worked for a young friend, assisting him in a fledgling import-export business. When that failed, he worked for another friend in the dry cleaning business, where he sometimes even mended clothes. It was on the basis of his meager salary at this last job, rather than on his salary at Mitsui, that his social security benefits were determined for the remainder of his life. My mother's benefits came to about $30 a month, and she cherished that small amount as "a gift from the government," using it carefully for special occasions and for money orders to supplement the dozens of packages my parents sent to friends and relatives in Japan for many years following the war.

In 1951, almost ten years after their lives had been decimated by the war and their forced removal, my parents were able to purchase a house with the help of my sister, who left New York City to live with them and work at the YWCA in Oakland as program director. The house was just two blocks from the one they first rented in 1917, but this time no one came to ask them to leave. My sister stayed with them a year and then left for Connecticut to marry a professor of mathematics at Yale University.

The Circle Is Completed

In the meantime, I spent two years in Japan as a Ford Foundation Foreign Area Fellow and became acquainted with the relatives and friends who until then had been only strangers to me. I often surprised and amused them by using old-fashioned Japanese words and phrases taught me by my Meiji Era parents, who had also instilled in me values and thoughts far more traditional than those held by some of my Japanese contemporaries. . . .

My experience in Japan was as positive and restorative as the evacuation had been negative and depleting. I came home aware of a new dimension to myself as a Japanese American and with new respect and admiration for the culture that had made my parents what they were. The circle was complete.

I feel grateful today for the Japanese values and traditions they instilled in me and kept alive in our home, and unlike the days of my youth, I am proud to be a Japanese American and am secure in that knowledge of myself.

I returned from Japan not knowing how long I would remain with my parents, but stayed to care for them in their declining years and to give them what comfort and sustenance I could.

In his seventy-sixth year my father suffered a stroke that left him partially paralyzed. But in the remaining ten years of his life, he learned to write with his left hand, continued to correspond with many friends, and did not abandon his annual campaign to raise funds for Doshisha University's Department of Theology, which his Issei friends supported generously. He and my mother faithfully attended Sycamore Congregational Church each Sunday, and joined its members in a fundraising drive that enabled the church to build a new sanctuary only sixteen years after the Japanese Americans returned from the camps to begin their new lives in California. When my mother died in 1966, my father endured her death with more strength than my sister or I. He had helped so many families through so many deaths, he knew what had to be done, and from his wheelchair he quietly and resolutely made all the necessary decisions.

My parents, like many of their Issei friends, did not fear death, for they had faced it so often and accepted it as a part of life. Both of them planned their own funeral services long before their deaths, selecting their favorite Japanese hymns and Bible verses. My mother wanted only a small family funeral and a memorial service for her friends, but my father wanted the customary evening funeral service held for most Issei. We followed both their wishes.

Understanding the Japanese Experience in America

The wartime evacuation of the Japanese Americans has already been well documented in many fine scholarly books. My story is a very personal one, and I speak only for myself and of those Issei and Nisei who were in the realm of my own experience, aware that they are only a small part of a larger whole. The story of my family is not typical of all Japanese immigrant families, and the lives of many other Japanese Americans were undoubtedly touched with more wartime tragedy and heartache than my own.

Still, there are many young Americans who have never heard about the evacuation or known of its effect on one Japanese American family. I hope the details of the life of my family, when added to those of others, will enhance their understanding of the history of the Japanese in California and enable them to see it as a vital element in that glorious and complex story of the immigrants from all lands who made America their home.

If my story has been long in coming, it is not because I did not want to remember our incarceration or to make this interior journey into my earlier self, but because it took so many years for these words to find a home. I am grateful that at last they have.

Today as a writer of books for young people, I often speak at schools about my experiences as a Japanese American. I want the children to perceive me not as a foreigner, as some still do, or as the stereotypic Asian they often see on film and television, but as a human being. I tell them of my pride in being a Japanese American today, but I also tell them I celebrate our common humanity, for I feel we must never lose our sense of connection with the human race. I tell them how it was to grow up as a Japanese American in California. I tell them about the Issei who persevered in a land that denied them so much. I tell them how our own country incarcerated us—its citizens—during World War II, causing us to lose that most precious of all possessions, our freedom.

"So It Won't Ever Happen Again"

The children ask me many questions, most of them about my wartime experiences. "I never knew we had concentration camps in America," one child told me in astonishment. "I thought they were only in Germany and Russia."

And so the story of the wartime incarceration of the Japanese Americans, as painful as it may be to hear, needs to be told and retold and never forgotten by succeeding generations of Americans.

I always ask the children why they think I wrote *Journey to Topaz* and *Journey Home*, in which I tell of the wartime experiences of the Japanese Americans. "To tell about the camps?" they ask. "To tell how you felt? To tell what happened to the Japanese people?"

"Yes," I answer, but I continue the discussion until finally one of them will say, "You wrote those books so it won't ever happen again."

And that is why I wrote this book. I wrote it for the young Japanese Americans who seek a sense of continuity with their past. But I wrote it as well for all Americans, with the hope that through knowledge of the past, they will never allow another group of people in America to be sent into a desert exile ever again.

Return to Minidoka

Monica Sone

In the following essay, Monica Sone, an internee at the
Minidoka relocation center in Idaho, relates the story of her
release by the War Relocation Authority (WRA). Second generation Japanese Americans [Nisei] who applied to college or
were able to find jobs and housing were permitted to resettle
in the Midwest and the East by the WRA. Though still not
permitted to return to the West Coast, Sone was enthusiastic
about getting a chance to start her life over in the midwest.
Two years after enrolling in Wendell College in southern
Indiana, Sone returned to the Minidoka camp to visit her parents, who were planning to return to the family hotel in Seattle, Washington, following their own release. During the visit,
Sone realized how the relocation, though horrible in many
respects, did help her come to terms with her Japanese roots.
Sone writes that she was no longer ashamed of her Japanese
ancestry and the relocation helped her to confidently claim
her place as an American citizen of Japanese descent.

I Enrolled at Wendell College in southern Indiana. The
cluster of ivy-covered red brick buildings stood gathered
on the edge of a thick-wooded bluff which rose almost three
hundred feet, overlooking the stately Ohio River. Wendell
College was a Presbyterian-affiliated liberal arts school, and
the atmosphere of its campus reflected a leisurely pace of
life, simplicity and friendly charm. Young people from all
walks of life were there . . . studying for the ministry, the
teaching profession, the medical profession and other var-

ied fields. There was also a distinct international air with foreign students from all parts of the world: South America, China, Java, India.

Mrs. Ashford, the widow with whom I lived on the edge of the campus, was an example of the college town's friendliness. She was a comfortable, motherly woman with silky, honey-colored hair done up in a bun, and merry blue eyes. Her husband had been a minister and college official. He had died several years before, and Mrs. Ashford had been living alone ever since. In the tall, two-storied gray frame house, my new friend had prepared a cozy room for me upstairs, where I could study quietly. Despite a stiff knee, Mrs. Ashford was up at dawn to fire up the furnace and prepare breakfast. I awakened to her cheerful call and the fragrant aroma of coffee wafting up to my room. In the evenings when I returned home from school, we sat in the two wooden rocking chairs in the sitting room, chatted about the days' events, listened to a favorite radio program or two, then I went upstairs to study. And always before bedtime, Mrs. Ashford called me down to the kitchen for a light snack because she firmly believed that mental work was just as exhausting as physical labor. Thus she provided me with the companionship I needed and a wealth of enchanting memories which I could conjure up at the thought of Wendell . . . the warm fragrance of freshly baked nutbread and homemade cookies filling the house on a cold winter night, the creaking porch swing where I could relax on warm spring evenings to watch the fireflies pinpoint the dark blue night, as I breathed in the thick sweet scent of lilacs surrounding the house.

There were three other Nisei girls enrolled at Wendell. Two were from southern California, and the third from my own home town. Faculty and students alike went out of their way to make us feel a real part of the campus life. We were swept into a round of teas and dinner parties, and invited to join the independent women's organization. The sororities included us in their rush parties, too, although because of a national ruling we could not be asked to join. I knew about this policy, and although I had ceased to feel personally hurt about it, one sorority apparently felt troubled by the restriction imposed on it. One day its officers, Alice Week, Lorraine Brown and the faculty advisor, Miss Knight, paid me a special visit. I remember how Alice looked at Miss Knight as if she were taking a deep breath before the plunge, and then spoke gently to me. "Monica, we've enjoyed meeting you, and we hope we'll get to know a lot more of each other from now on. But there are national restrictions placed on our membership. Although many of us sincerely want to invite you into our group, we can't. I hope you understand."

After a moment of embarrassed silence, I managed to say, "Yes, Alice, I do know about this from back home. I understand."

Lorraine said, "We felt we should tell you about it, Monica, rather than say nothing. We didn't want you to think we were ignoring you for personal reasons."

"Thank you. I really appreciate your visit." I knew this call had cost them something in pride, and it took moral honesty to have come in the spirit in which they did. . . .

Life at Wendell

The professors were at once friendly and casual. Although during class hours they were distant and insistent that we study, we grew to know them, their wives and their children, well at school and church functions and from day-to-day encounters at the post office and stores. There was one distinguished-looking language professor whom I always called whenever I wanted to get a ride into town on a Saturday. Dr. Konig and his wife always went into town on week ends, taking a carload of students with them. There was another, tall, gruff-mannered economics professor whom we could sometimes persuade to move classes out to the cool green lawn under the trees on warm spring days. And whenever I was faced with a vexing personal problem, I immediately hied myself to Dr. or Mrs. Scott who diffused affection and understanding like a glowing hearth fire. It was a far cry from the dignified and austere University of

Washington where I hurried alone from class to class along the sprawling pathways.

I had been intimidated by the racial barriers in the business and professional world and I wasn't brave enough to explore or develop my other interests. It seemed useless to do so in the face of closed doors. So when I entered the University of Washington, I clung to literature, my first love, saying to my friends that I wanted to teach. We all knew this was a fancy, too, destined to wither.

Now my interests exploded in a number of directions—music, history and current events, religion and philosophy, sociology. But above all, I discovered that I liked people, as individuals and unique personalities. Whatever career I chose, it would have something to do with people. And since I had to come to the Midwest and was embarked on a life more normal and happier than I had dared hope for, I gradually uncoiled and relaxed enough to take more honest stock of my real inclinations. I was attracted to psychology courses and did well in them. After talking it over with my advisor, I decided to go into Clinical Psychology. . . .

Return to Minidoka

My second year at Wendell, just before Christmas, I had a letter from Father and Mother, who were still in camp, urging me to spend the holiday with them. "It would be so nice to have at least one of you back." They enclosed a check for the railroad fare. So I packed a suitcase, kissed Mrs. Ashford "Good-by and Merry Christmas," and set off for Camp Minidoka. . . .

At Camp Minidoka, I was startled to see an MP [military policeman] again, standing at the gate. I had forgotten about such things as MP's and barbed-wire fences. Mother rushed out of the gate shelter, her face beaming. "Ka-chan! It was so good of you to come. Have you been well and happy?" She looked closely into my face. I was relieved to see Mother looking well and still full of smiles, although I noticed a few gray streaks in her smooth jet-black head of hair as I hugged her.

"Where's Papa?" I asked.

"He had a bad cold, and he's resting at the hospital now. He'll be home in a day or two."

Although Mother tried to hide it, I learned that Father had had a close brush with pneumonia.

The camp was quiet and ghostly, drained of its young blood. All of the able-bodied Nisei men had been drafted into the army. The rest of the young people had relocated to the Midwest and East to jobs and schools. Some of the parents had followed them out. But the Issei [first generation Japanese Americans] who still wanted to go back West and had a home or a business to return to, remained in camp, hoping that the military restriction on the Coast would be lifted at the end of the war.

When I stepped into our old barracks room, I felt as if I had returned to a shell of a prison. The room had been stripped down to two cots, and it yawned silent and bare. The white walls were now filmed over with a dingy gray from the coal smoke. The wall where Sumi's cot had stood, formerly plastered with movie actors' pictures, was empty and dotted with black pinholes. The dressing table, once cluttered with rows of nail polishes, lipsticks and bottles of cologne, stood stark and empty. Only Mother and Father's brush and comb sets lay there, neatly, side by side.

That evening Mother and I went to see Father at the hospital. From a distance down the hall I could see him sitting up in bed. What had been a firm-fleshed, nut-brown face, was now thin-chiseled and pinched. His high forehead gleamed pale. I did not have the heart to ask whether this was only the result of his illness.

I had written to Father and Mother about everything which had happened to me since I left camp, but they wanted to hear about it all over again. For two hours I talked, telling them in detail about the Richardson family, how I had been able to return to school, and about my new friends at Wendell. Mother had been studying me as I talked. She said, "You've become a happy person, Ka-chan. I remember those days back in Seattle when the war started, I wondered when any of us would ever feel secure and happy again. We worried a great deal about our children."

"At Least I Still Have the Business"

Father told me that things were not going too well with his business in Seattle. From the looks of the monthly reports, Father suspected that somebody was siphoning huge sums of money into his own pockets, and juggling books to make it appear that vast improvements were being made, which Father had no way of checking. Father said that Henry was going to Seattle soon to look into the matter. Henry had given up thoughts of pursuing his medical career for the present, and he and Minnie decided to leave St. Louis and go back to Seattle to help Father with his business comeback. Minnie's folks planned to return to their former home, too.

"At least I still have the business," Father said philosophically. "I'm a lot luckier than many of my friends who lost everything."

Mr. Kato had lost his hotel lease and his entire personal property had been carted away from the hotel by men, posing as government storage men, who said they were going to move everything into the storehouse. Mr. Kato and his wife said they would probably work together as houseman and cook in a home, for a while, when they returned to Seattle until they had a better plan. For the present, they were waiting their days out, looking for mail from their son Jiro who was somewhere in Europe.

Mr. Oshima had been released from the internment camp in Missoula. He and his wife intended to return to the barber business provided they could find a suitable shop. They were living in suspended anxiety for their son Dunks had been taken prisoner of war by the Germans. . . .

Father asked me to call on his best friend, Mr. Sawada, the former clothes salesman. "He's all alone here now since his daughter has left for Chicago. As you know, George was killed in Italy, and now his other son, Paul, is reported missing in action. Mr. Sawada often asks about you." I remembered long ago how hard Mr. Sawada had worked to send

George to medical school, and how he straightened up whenever he talked about his children.

"I'll Be Happy in Seattle"

I found Mr. Sawada in an untidy room. Half-filled teacups stood on windowsills and a saucer overflowed with cigarette butts. An odd wired cage stood on a stool near the stove, a ragged gray sweater flung over it. Mr. Sawada grinned as he caught me staring at it. "This is where Shozo lives," he said. He pulled the sweater off to show me a disgruntled black crow. "For hours I sat out there on the prairie before I could persuade him to light on my shoulder. Since then we've become good friends. Sometimes I let him fly around in here, but he gets it so messy. I think one messy old man in the room is enough, don't you?"

I laughed. Mr. Sawada was still his cheerful, casual self. He told me he was eager to return to Seattle. When I said that I didn't want to go back there for a long, long time, he said, "You young ones feel everything so keenly. It's good, but sometimes you must suffer more for it. When you get old like me, Kazuko-san, things are not so sharply differentiated into black and white. Don't worry, I'll be happy in Seattle. The common people there won't hold grudges for long, and neither will I. All the fire and emotion will have died down. All I want is to live out my days there peacefully."

We sat silently together for a moment. Then I stood up to leave. "It was nice seeing you again, Mr. Sawada. Please take good care of yourself, and I hope you will hear good news about Paul soon."

"Hah, *arigato*. I'm praying."

"And I was terribly sorry to hear about George."

Mr. Sawada said quietly, "He walked into it, that boy of mine. Maybe you heard . . . he volunteered to go on a special mission."

"Yes, Father told me about it."

I lapsed into an unhappy silence, thinking how painful it must be for him to talk about it. He spoke to me gently, as if he were trying to put me at ease. "Kazuko-san, I want to show you a letter which he wrote me when he was on the train, on his way to Camp Shelby. After you read it, you will understand why I do not feel as lonely as you think I do." He walked to a bookshelf on which stood a photograph of George in uniform. A Japanese Bible lay in front of it. From between its pages, Mr. Sawada withdrew the letter and handed it to me.

"This Is Your Sacrifice"

In the quiet of the little room where I heard only the loud ticking of the alarm clock and Shozo strutting up and down on his horny little feet, I read George's letter, written only a few hours after he had told his father good-by at the camp gate.

He wrote: "I feel I owe it to myself and to you to tell you some of the things I should have said and didn't when the time came for us to part. I don't know why I didn't. Perhaps, because I was overly reticent; perhaps, it was because we were Japanese, but mainly, because I think I was a little bit self-conscious."

George went on to say that as the train carried him away, he was thinking back over their happy family life. He recalled family picnics, the sorrow when his mother died, the family struggles and triumphs. "When Evacuation Day came," George wrote, "I was stricken with bitterness, and I remember how you comforted me. I could not then understand why you tried to restore my faith in this country which was now rejecting us, making us penniless. You said wisely: 'It is for the best. For the good of many, a few must suffer. This is your sacrifice. Accept it as such and you will no longer be bitter.' I listened, and my bitterness left me. You, who had never been allowed citizenship, showed me its value. That I retained my faith and emerged a loyal American citizen, I owe to your understanding. When the time came for enlistment, I was ready."

There were tears in my eyes. I heard Mr. Sawada say, "With this letter, George will comfort me always. I know that George understood and loved me well."

I thanked him for letting me read the letter. He took Shozo

out of the cage and walked to the door with me. "Well, Kazuko-san, study hard. But don't forget to keep one eye out for your future husband!"

I laughed, in spite of my brimming eyes, and walked quickly away.

"Two Heads Are Better than One"

The days passed by too quickly and it was time to leave Camp Minidoka. Father and Mother accompanied me to the camp gate. It was one of those crisp winter mornings when the pale sky and the snow were bathed in a taut cold pink.

"Ah, well, this parting is not a sad one for us, is it, Mama?" Father said. "It isn't as if she were a young son going off to war."

"This is what happens to all parents. Children grow, and they must fly away. But it is well . . . you all seem so happy in your letters, Henry and Minnie in St. Louis, and Sumi way out there in the East. When the war came and we were all evacuated, Papa and I were heartsick. We felt terribly bad about being your Japanese parents."

"No, don't say those things, Mama, please. If only you knew how much I have changed about being a Nisei. It wasn't such a tragedy. I don't resent my Japanese blood anymore. I'm proud of it, in fact, because of you and the Issei who've struggled so much for us. It's really nice to be born into two cultures, like getting a real bargain in life, two for the price of one. The hardest part, I guess, is the growing up, but after that, it can be interesting and stimulating. I used to feel like a two-headed monstrosity, but now I find that two heads are better than one."

Father beamed, "It makes us very happy to hear that."

"In spite of the war and the mental tortures we went through, I think the Nisei have attained a clearer understanding of America and its way of life, and we have learned to value her more. Her ideas and ideals of democracy are based essentially on religious principles and her very existence depends on the faith and moral responsibilities of each individual. I used to think of the government as a paternal organization. When it failed me, I felt bitter and sullen. Now I know I'm just as responsible as the men in Washington for its actions. Somehow it all makes me feel much more at home in America. All in all, I think the Issei's losses during this war are greater."

"If we consider material losses, maybe so, but our children's gain is our gain, too. Our deepest happiness we receive from our children," Father said.

Returning to Seattle

"What are you and Mama going to do, the first thing after you return to Seattle?"

Father had a ready reply.

"Oh, first, we'll go and say 'Hello and thank you' to Joe, Sam and Peter for looking after the hotel. After that, we will take a walk along the waterfront and maybe dine on a crab or two. Then we will buy a little house and wait for visits from you all with your little children."

Mother smiled in assent. I gave a quick hug to Father and Mother and stepped inside the bus. As I looked out of the window, I saw them standing patiently, wrapped in heavy dark winter clothes, Father in his old navy pea jacket, Mother in black wool slacks and black coat. They looked like wistful immigrants. I wondered when they would be able to leave their no-man's land, pass through the legal barrier and become naturalized citizens. Then I thought, in America, many things are possible. When I caught Father and Mother's eyes, they smiled instantly.

I was returning to Wendell College with confidence and hope. I had discovered a deeper, stronger pulse in the American scene. I was going back into its main stream, still with my Oriental eyes, but with an entirely different outlook, for now I felt more like a whole person instead of a sadly split personality. The Japanese and the American parts of me were now blended into one.

Chronology

1890s
The first Japanese immigrants arrive in the United States. Judged incapable of assimilating into American society, they are prohibited from becoming citizens.

1913
California passes the Alien-Land Act, prohibiting land ownership by aliens ineligible for citizenship.

1924
Congress passes the National Origins Act, barring immigration by aliens ineligible for citizenship.

1940
The Census finds 126,947 Japanese in the United States; 79,642 are native-born citizens.

December 7, 1941
The Japanese attack the American Pacific Fleet at Pearl Harbor, Hawaii, and launch offensives against the Philippines and Hong Kong; authorized by a blanket presidential warrant, Attorney General Francis Biddle directs the FBI to arrest a predetermined number of "enemy aliens" classified as dangerous. Among those arrested are 737 Japanese.

December 8, 1941
The United States declares war on Japan.

December 11, 1941
1,370 Japanese classified as "dangerous enemy aliens" are detained by the FBI.

December 29, 1941

All enemy aliens in California, Oregon, Washington, Montana, Idaho, Utah, and Nevada are ordered to surrender all contraband. Contraband includes radios with short wave bands, cameras, binoculars, and a variety of weapons.

January 5, 1942

All Japanese American selective service registrants are placed in Class 4-C along with enemy aliens. Japanese Americans already in military service are discharged or assigned menial tasks.

January 6, 1942

Los Angeles congressman Leland Ford sends a telegram to Secretary of State Cordell Hull urging the removal of all Japanese from the West Coast.

January 28, 1942

The California State Personnel Board votes to bar all descendants of enemy aliens from civil service positions. This rule is enforced only against persons of Japanese ancestry.

January 29, 1942

Attorney General Biddle issues the first of a series of orders establishing prohibited zones which must be cleared of all enemy aliens. German, Japanese, and Italian aliens are instructed to evacuate areas on the San Francisco waterfront.

February 4, 1942

The U.S. Army defines twelve "restricted areas." Enemy aliens in these designated areas must observe a curfew (9 P.M. to 6 A.M.) and are allowed to travel only to and from work. In addition, they are forbidden to travel any further than five miles from their place of residence.

February 13, 1942

The West Coast congressional delegation sends a letter to President Roosevelt urging the removal of persons of Japanese ancestry, aliens and citizens alike, from strategic areas of California, Oregon, and Washington.

February 16, 1942
FBI arrests or detains a reported 2,192 Japanese aliens.

February 19, 1942
Roosevelt signs Executive Order 9066 authorizing the military evacuation and internment of 110,000 Japanese Americans from the West Coast.

February 20, 1942
Secretary of War Henry L. Stimson appoints Lieutenant General John L. DeWitt as the military commander responsible for executing Executive Order 9066.

February 21, 1942
Hearings by the House Select Committee Investigating National Defense Migration (the Tolan Committee) begin on the West Coast to investigate problems of enemy aliens living along the Pacific coast.

February 23, 1942
A Japanese submarine shells an oil refinery in Goleta, California, just outside of Santa Barbara. No injuries are reported.

February 25, 1942
The army fires thousands of anti-aircraft rounds at an unidentified target near Santa Monica, California. The object was later determined to be a lost weather balloon and the incident becomes known as "The Battle of Los Angeles."

February 28, 1942
General DeWitt issues Public Proclamation Number One designating military areas in Washington, Oregon, California, and Arizona, from which aliens of Japanese, German, and Italian ancestry may be excluded.

March 6, 1942

The Federal Reserve Bank is designated as a cooperation agency to help persons being evacuated to dispose of their property or make arrangements to administer property left behind.

March 16, 1942

General DeWitt issues Public Proclamation Number Two, designating Idaho, Montana, Nevada, and Utah as Military Areas Three through Six.

March 18, 1942

President Roosevelt signs Executive Order 9102. The Executive Order creates the War Relocation Authority (WRA) to implement a program of orderly evacuation of designated persons from restricted areas.

March 23, 1942

General DeWitt issues Civilian Exclusion Order Number One, directing all persons of Japanese ancestry, both aliens and American citizens, to evacuate Bainbridge Island near Seattle, Washington, before March 30.

March 24, 1942

General DeWitt issues Public Proclamation Number Four, extending travel restrictions, curfew, and contraband regulations to all persons of Japanese ancestry regardless of citizenship.

May 8, 1942

The evacuation of all Japanese living within the Arizona Military Area is completed.

July 13, 1942

Mitsuye Endo files a writ of habeas corpus asking the government to release her from her relocation center or show just cause as to why she should continue to be kept in custody.

August 7, 1942
General DeWitt announces that the removal of 110,000 persons of Japanese ancestry from Military Areas Number One and Two is complete.

October 1, 1942
WRA allows select evacuees to seek temporary or permanent residence outside the relocation centers.

November 3, 1942
Final group of evacuees from California reaches Jerome, Arkansas. The Army transfers direct jurisdiction of evacuees to the WRA, except for those evacuees who remain in West Coast institutions.

November 18, 1942
Evacuees at the Poston Relocation Center in Arizona protest the arrest of two evacuees accused of beating a third who was thought to be a camp informer.

November 23, 1942
A general strike is called at Poston.

December 6, 1942
Violence breaks out at the Manzanar Relocation Center in California. Military police fire into a crowd, killing two evacuees and wounding at least ten others.

January 28, 1943
The privilege of volunteering for military service is restored to the Nisei (children of Japanese immigrants who were citizens by benefit of birth in the United States). Over 2,500 men volunteer for service.

February 3, 1943
The WRA begins administering a loyalty questionnaire to all evacuees over seventeen years of age; the 442nd Regimental Combat Team is officially activated by the U.S.

Army. The Unit is initially made up of the 100th Battalion from Hawaii and Japanese American volunteers from the mainland. This unit fights bravely in North Africa, Italy, France, and later in Germany.

June 4, 1943
America's naval victory over Japan in the Battle of Midway cripples Japan's ability to wage an offensive naval war, ending the Japanese threat to the West Coast.

July 31, 1943
The Tule Lake Relocation Center is designated as a segregation camp for disloyal evacuees by the WRA.

November 1, 1943
The U.S. Army assumes control of the Tule Lake Relocation Center, resulting in mass demonstrations by the evacuees.

January 14, 1944
U.S. Army's control of Tule Lake is terminated.

January 20, 1944
Secretary of War Stimson announces that Japanese Americans are again eligible for the draft.

June 30, 1944
The Jerome Relocation Center in Arkansas becomes the first of the relocation centers to close. The 5,000 remaining evacuees are transferred to other camps.

December 17, 1944
Major General Henry C. Pratt, acting commander of the Western Defense Command, issues Public Proclamation Number Twenty-one which restores the rights of evacuees to return to their former homes; all contraband regulations are lifted.

December 18, 1944
The Supreme Court upholds Executive Order 9066 in *Korematsu v. United States.* In a separate ruling, the Court finds in favor of Mitsuye Endo and rules that the WRA cannot detain loyal citizens nor prevent them from returning to the West Coast.

December 30, 1944
The WRA announces the opening of relocation offices in Seattle, San Francisco, and Los Angeles. These offices are to assist evacuees returning to the West Coast.

August 6, 1945
The United States drops an atomic bomb on Hiroshima, Japan.

August 9, 1945
The United States drops a second atomic bomb on Nagasaki, Japan.

August 14, 1945
Japan surrenders to the Allies.

September 4, 1945
The Western Defense Command revokes all restrictions against Japanese and Japanese Americans.

March 20, 1946
The Tule Lake Relocation Center is closed. All relocation centers are now empty.

June 30, 1946
The WRA is deactivated.

1980
Congress creates the Commission on Wartime Relocation and Internment of Civilians to review the circumstances surrounding Executive Order 9066. The Commission concludes

that the removal of Japanese residents from the West Coast was not justified and recommends that restitution be made to the survivors of the relocation.

1990
President George Bush issues a formal apology to former internees; the first reparations checks are mailed to survivors of the relocation camps.

For Further Research

Leonard J. Arrington, *The Price of Prejudice: The Japanese-American Relocation Center in Utah During World War II.* Logan: Utah State University Press, 1962.

Paul Bailey, *City in the Sun: The Japanese Concentration Camp at Poston, Arizona.* Los Angeles: Westernlore Press, 1971.

Lillian Baker, ed., *Dishonoring America: The Collective Guilt of American Japanese.* Lawndale, CA: Americans for Historical Accuracy, 1988.

Allan R. Bosworth, *America's Concentration Camps.* New York: W.W. Norton, 1967.

Gordon H. Chang, ed., *Morning Glory, Evening Shadow: Yamato Ichihashi and His Internment Writings, 1942–1945.* Stanford, CA: Stanford University Press, 1997.

Commission on Wartime Relocation and Internment of Civilians, *Personal Justice Denied.* Washington, DC: GPO, 1982.

Roger Daniels, *Prisoners Without Trial: Japanese-Americans in World War II.* New York: Hill and Wang, 1993.

Roger Daniels, ed., *American Concentration Camps: A Documentary History of the Relocation and Incarceration of Japanese-Americans, 1942–1945.* New York: Garland Press, 1989.

Roger Daniels, Sandra C. Taylor, and Harry H.L. Kitano, eds., *Japanese Americans: From Relocation to Redress.* Salt Lake City: University of Utah Press, 1983.

Daniel S. Davis, *Behind Barbed Wire.* New York: E.P. Dutton, 1982.

Louis Fiset, *Imprisoned Apart: The World War II Correspondence of an Issei Couple*. Seattle: University of Washington Press, 1997.

Anne Reeploeg Fisher, *Exile of a Race*. Seattle: F&T Publishers, 1965.

Audrey Girdner and Anne Loftis, *The Great Betrayal: The Evacuation of the Japanese-Americans During World War II*. New York: Macmillan, 1969.

Morton Grodzins, *Americans Betrayed: Politics and the Japanese Evacuation*. Chicago: University of Chicago Press, 1949.

Arthur A. Hansen, ed., *Japanese American World War II Evacuation Oral History Project, parts 1–5*. Westport, CT: Meckler, 1991.

Lane Ryo Hirabayashi, ed., *Inside an American Concentration Camp: Japanese American Resistance at Poston, Arizona*. Tucson: University of Arizona Press, 1995.

Bill Hosokawa, *Out of the Frying Pan: Recollections of a Japanese American*. Niwot: University of Colorado Press, 1998.

Jeanne Wakatsuki Houston and James D. Houston, *Farewell to Manzanar*. New York: Bantam Books, 1973.

Daisuke Kitagawa, *Issei and Nisei: The Internment Years*. New York: Seabury Press, 1967.

Toru Matsumoto, *Beyond Prejudice*. New York: Arno Press, 1978.

John Modell, ed., *The Kikuchi Diary: Chronicle from an American Concentration Camp: The Tanforan Journals of Charles Kikuchi*. Urbana: University of Illinois Press, 1973.

Dillon S. Myer, *Uprooted Americans: The Japanese Americans and the War Relocation Authority During World War II*. Tucson: University of Arizona Press, 1971.

Douglas W. Nelson, *Heart Mountain: The Story of an American Concentration Camp*. Madison: State Historical Society of Wisconsin, 1976.

Mine Okubo, *Citizen 13660*. New York: Columbia University Press, 1966.

Page Smith, *Democracy on Trial*. New York: Simon & Schuster, 1995.

Monica Sone, *Nisei Daughter*. Boston: Little, Brown, 1953.

John Tateishi, ed., *And Justice for All: An Oral History of the Japanese American Detention Camps*. Seattle: University of Washington Press, 1984.

Yoshiko Uchida, *Desert Exile: The Uprooting of a Japanese American Family*. Seattle: University of Washington Press, 1982.

Michi Weglyn, *Years of Infamy: The Untold Story of America's Concentration Camps*. New York: Morrow Quill, 1976.

Index